SUSSEX
Teashop Walks

Jean Patefield

D1079093

COUNTRYSIDE BOOKS
NEWBURY BERKSHIRE

First published 2000
© Jean Patefield 2000

All rights reserved.
No reproduction permitted without the
prior permission of the publisher:

COUNTRYSIDE BOOKS
3 Catherine Road
Newbury, Berkshire

To view our complete range of books,
please visit us at
www.countrysidebooks.co.uk

ISBN 1 85306 623 0

Designed by Graham Whiteman
Cover illustration by Colin Doggett
Photographs and maps by the author

Produced through MRM Associates Ltd., Reading
Typeset by Techniset Typesetters, Newton-le-Willows
Printed by Woolnough Bookbinding Ltd., Irthlingborough

Contents

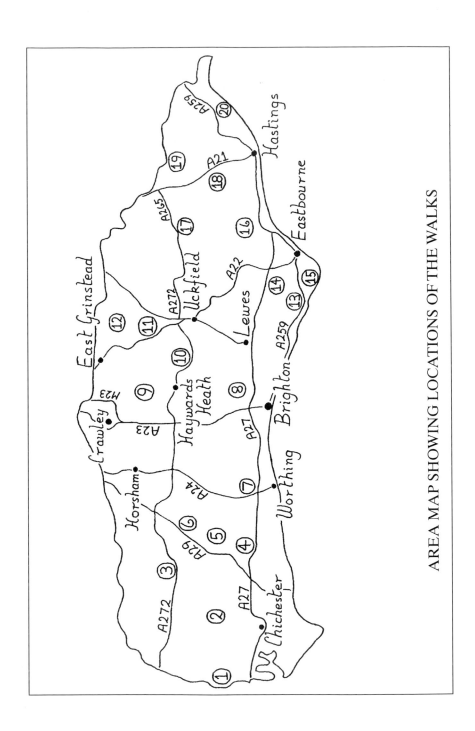

AREA MAP SHOWING LOCATIONS OF THE WALKS

Walk

Introduction

The poet Tennyson, who lived at Aldworth House in the north-west corner of the county, wrote of 'green Sussex fading into blue with one grey glimpse of sea'. Do not be misled into thinking of Sussex as a vast commuter sprawl. It remains a largely rural county with a great variety of landscapes and excellent walking. The tea shops are outstanding – and I speak as one who knows!

Tea is not only refreshing during a walk; it is good for you! In Scotland apothecaries sold it and it was available on prescription on form number 99. This is the origin of the name of one famous brand. Another, Typhoo, is the Chinese word for doctor.

Tea is often said to be the best meal to eat out in England and I believe it is a meal to be enjoyed on all possible occasions. The custom of afternoon tea is said to have been invented by Anna, Duchess of Bedford, in about 1840. She often became peckish in the late afternoon – don't we all? – and invited her friends to join her in a snack of sandwiches and cake. Scones with clotted cream and strawberry jam, delicious home made cakes, toasted teacakes dripping with butter in winter, delicate cucumber sandwiches in summer all washed down with the cup that cheers are some of the best, typically English foods available and often excellent value. Bad for the figure maybe, but the walking will see to that.

The best tea shops serve a range of cakes, all home made and including fruit cake as well as scones and other temptations. Teapots should be capacious and pour properly. Many of the tea shops visited on these walks fulfil all these criteria admirably and they all offer a good tea. They always have at least light lunches available as well so there is no need to think of these walks as just something for the afternoons.

There is an abundance of excellent establishments in Sussex but even so, tea shops are not scattered evenly throughout the county. In some places popular with tourists, the visitor is spoilt for choice. In such cases the most convenient tea shop that, in the author's opinion, most closely fulfils the criteria set out above is recommended but should that not appeal, there are others from which to choose. In other places where there is a delightful walk to be enjoyed, the choice for tea is more limited. However, they all offer a good tea part way round an attractive walk. The opening times and telephone number of each tea shop are given. Some are rather vague about when they open out of season: it seems to depend on weather and mood. If you are planning a walk on a wet November Tuesday, for example, a call to check that tea will actually be available that day is a wise precaution. A few are definitely closed in the depths of winter and for these walks an alternative source of refreshment is given. In most cases, these are pubs serving food, which in some cases includes tea.

The pleasures of summer walking are obvious. Many of the teashops featured in this book have an attractive garden where tea can be taken outside when the weather is suitable. However, let me urge you not to overlook the pleasures of a good walk in winter. The roads and paths are quieter and what could be better than sitting by an open fire in a cosy teashop scoffing crumpets that you can enjoy with a clear conscience due to the brisk walk to get them!

The 20 walks in this book explore the varied landscapes of Sussex. They are all between 3 and 7½ miles long and should be well within the capacity of the average person, including those of mature years and families with children. They are intended to take the walker through this attractive corner of England at a gentle pace with plenty of time to stop and stare, to savour the beauty and interest all around. A dedicated yomper and stomper could probably knock off the whole book in a single weekend but in doing so they would have missed the point and seen nothing. To fully appreciate the countryside it is necessary to go slowly with your eyes and ears open.

Some of the walks are short and level, ideal for a pipe opener on a winter's day, or giving plenty of time to dawdle away a summer's afternoon. Others are longer or more strenuous, some making an excellent all day expedition. Certain of the walks involve some climbing. This is inevitable as hills add enormous interest to the countryside and with no hills there are no views. However, this presents no problem to the sensible walker who has three uphill gears – slowly, very slowly and admiring the view. None of the walks in this book are inherently hazardous but sensible care should be taken. Many of the falls that do happen are due to unsuitable footwear, since grass slopes can be as slippery as the more obviously hazardous wet, smooth rock. Proper walking shoes or boots also give some protection to the ankle. It is also essential to look where you are putting your feet to avoid tripping up. Wainwright, the doyen of walkers in the Lake District, said that he never had a serious fall in all his years and thousands of miles of walking because he always looked where he put his feet and stopped if he wanted to admire the scenery.

All the routes are on public rights of way or permissive paths and have been carefully checked but, of course, in the countryside things do change; a stile replaces a gate or a wood is extended. A map illustrates each walk and they are all circular. An Ordnance Survey map is useful as well, especially for identifying the main features of views. The area is covered by Landranger 1:50,000 (1¼ inches to 1 mile) series sheets, 187, 188, 189, 197,

198 and 199. Even better for walking are the 1:25,000 Explorer 120, 121, 122, 123, 124, 125, 133, 135 and 136. The grid reference of the starting point and the appropriate maps are given for each walk.

The walks are designed so that, starting where suggested, the teashop is reached in the second half so a really good appetite for tea can be worked up and then its effects walked off. Some walks start at a car park, which is ideal. Where this is not possible, the suggested starting place will always have somewhere a few cars can be left without endangering other traffic or causing inconvenience. However, it sometimes fits in better with the plans for the day to start and finish at the teashop and so for each walk there are details of how to do this.

So put on your walking shoes and prepare to be delighted by the charms of Sussex and refreshed by a traditional English tea!

Jean Patefield

KEY TO SKETCH MAPS

Path on route	— → —	Summit	△	Point in text	⑤
Path not on route	···	Church	†	Car Park	▢
Road	═══	Tea shop	☕	Building or feature referred to in text	▪
River or stream	∿∿∿				
Sea, lake or pond	⌒∼∼⌒	Pub referred to in text	PH	Railway	┼┼┼┼┼)(┼

Walk 1
STANSTED FOREST AND ROWLAND'S CASTLE

This walk explores the magnificent woods of the Stansted Estate. The paths are in Sussex and the tea shop lies a few yards over the border in Hampshire. When I wrote a book of tea shop walks in Hampshire a year or two ago, I left out this walk because it is almost entirely in Sussex. I am determined not to leave out this highly recommended route again because the tea shop is in Hampshire! County boundaries are, after all, merely lines on a map. Almost all this walk is in woodland and it is a joy at any time of year, The colours are wonderful in autumn and the signs of returning life in spring gladden the heart. The paths are shady on a hot summer's day and the shapes of the many magnificent trees are best appreciated in winter.

The Coffee Pot in Rowland's Castle overlooks the large, immaculate village green. There is an excellent selection of cakes, supplemented by super desserts including fruit pies and crumbles, bread pudding or trifle. For lunch there are filled jacket potatoes, sandwiches and stuffed pancakes as well as full meals, including a roast on Sunday. Walkers are positively welcomed at this friendly tea shop and there are tables outside at the front and in the garden at the side. The Coffee Pot is open throughout the year between 9 am and 5 pm, 10 am on Sundays. Telephone: 01705 412538.

DISTANCE: 5 miles.

MAP: OS Landranger 197 Chichester and the South Downs or Explorer 120 Chichester, South Harting and Selsey.

STARTING POINT: The most southerly of the Stansted Forest car parks (GR 754103).

HOW TO GET THERE: From the A271, Havant to Chichester road, at Emsworth take the B2147 to Westbourne. In Westbourne take a minor road, North Street, signed 'Rowlands Castle' and follow it through and out of the village for about a mile. At a T-junction turn right, signed 'Chichester'. After 200 yards turn left, signed 'Forestside 2 W. Marden 3' and 'Stansted House' to a car park on the left after about a mile.

ALTERNATIVE STARTING POINT: If you wish to visit the tea shop at the beginning or end of your walk, start in Rowland's Castle where there is a small car park opposite the Castle public house. The tea shop lies to the left under the railway arches. You will then start the walk at point 9, turning left out of the tea shop and following the road under the railway and past the Castle public house to a path on the right. Turn right along this to a cross track with an information board.

THE WALK

1. Return to the road and turn left for 100 yards then right on a surfaced drive in front of a pillared lodge. Ignore tracks on the left.

Ahead lies Stansted House. The first building on the site was a medieval hunting lodge built by the first Earl of Arundel. A large country house was built in 1688 but this burned down in 1900. It was rebuilt on the same spot in 1903 in sumptuous Christopher Wren style, complete with colonnaded portico, roof balustrades and a cupola perched on top. It is full of Bessborough family treasures but perhaps the most interesting part is the extensive servants' quarters showing how the many employees lived during the heyday of the English country house, before the First World War. The servants' quarters are open, together with the chapel and grounds, on summer afternoons except on Wednesday and Thursday and the rest of the

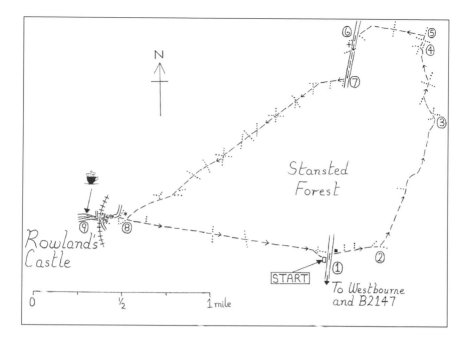

house, which finds a modern role in corporate hospitality and functions, is open on Sunday and Monday afternoons in July and August. Telephone: 01705 412265.

2. At the start of a wooden fence on the left, turn left through a small gate that leads alongside a wood. Follow this for about a mile, **ignoring a path over a stile on the left when the path briefly enters the wood after about ¹/₂ mile.**

3. The path bears left into the wood. Some 75 yards into the wood, bear left on a cross path, shown by a yellow arrow on a post, that shortly passes a chest-high wooden barrier. Look out for this junction as it is easily missed. Follow this path through the wood. Go over a cross path then bear left when the path forks after a further 30 yards.

4. Now watch for a path on the right. Do not take this but continue on for 25 yards to a cross path and turn right here, as shown by a yellow arrow on a post. Ignore all side turns and press on through the wood to a metal kissing gate out of the wood.

5. Do not go through the gate. Instead, turn left along the edge of

11

the wood, walking with a hedge on the right. Follow the path to a wooden kissing gate giving onto a road.

6. Turn left for quarter of a mile to a second signed path on the right.

7. Turn right. Pass a ride on the left and after a further 110 yards, bear left as indicated by a yellow way mark. Follow this path for about a mile, ignoring numerous cross paths: at most junctions, a yellow arrow on a post shows the correct path. The path joins a roughly surfaced track. Continue ahead, again ignoring side turns, as far as a cross path where there is a magnificent beech to the right opposite an information board on the left. *Note this point.

Stansted House is surrounded by over a thousand acres of woodland. The estate is now owned and managed by the Stansted Park Foundation. The last owner, the 10th Earl of Bessborough, made the estate over to this charitable trust charged with its preservation for the benefit of future generations.

8. Turn right to a road. Turn left into Rowland's Castle and the tea shop is on the right beyond the railway arches.

The road passes the Castle public house on the right. This was built to replace the White Hart, which had to be knocked down to make way for the railway arches in 1853. In the middle of the 18th century, this area was, 'infested with highwaymen, deerstalkers, smugglers and thieves'. Among this low-life was the Hawkhurst gang. In October 1747 they seized a large illicit shipment of tea from Poole customs house then rode through Fordingbridge to distribute it. One of them was recognised by Daniel Chater, an elderly shoemaker, who went to Chichester to give evidence and claim his reward. He was captured by the gang and brutally murdered at the White Hart. Many were horrified at the cruelty of the attack on an honest citizen and a reward was offered for the apprehension of the perpetrators. The gang was turned in and later hanged.

9. From the tea shop return to the beech tree and information board * and now go ahead over the track and a footbridge. Head up to a magnificent open ride with Stansted House in view at the end. The path lies along the left of the ride. As you approach a road, turn right on a cross path back to the car park. (If you started the walk at Rowland's Castle, go straight on and across the road.)

Walk 2
CHARLTON AND SINGLETON

Within living memory, expanses of downland have fallen under the plough. What was once a colourful, living tapestry of flowers supporting populations of insects and birds is now, all too often, a sterile carpet of cereals. This route is not long or demanding. It explores an important nature reserve that acts as a reminder of the way things used to be. In addition to the interesting natural history, the views alone are well worth the walk. After Levin Down, the route visits two downland villages, Charlton and Singleton, the latter with a charming tea room attached to an artist's studio, before a short walk returns you to the start.

Sue Martin set up Singleton Studio Tea Room as a tea room and craft gallery selling her own and her brothers' work. Particularly interesting is a collection of over 800 limited edition prints in the Portraits of Britain series depicting scenes from all corners of these islands. Increasing artistic success means Lynn Williams now runs the tea room. This charming establishment overlooking the village pond offers an excellent selection of delicious cakes, including unusual varieties such as a Victorian peach and fig cake. For lunch there are sandwiches and filled jacket potatoes as well as daily specials. The tea room is open every day throughout the summer between 10 am and 5 pm, extending to 5.30 pm at weekends. In winter it is open at weekends. Telephone: 01243 811899.

When the tea shop is closed, the pub in Singleton, the Fox and Hounds, serves food.

DISTANCE: 4¹/₂ miles.

MAP: OS Landranger 197 Chichester and the South Downs or Explorer 120 Chichester, South Harting and Selsey.

STARTING POINT: The parking area on the west side of the A286 ¹/₂ mile north of Singleton (GR 876139).

HOW TO GET THERE: The starting point is on the A286, Chichester to Midhurst road, ¹/₂ mile north of Singleton.

ALTERNATIVE STARTING POINT: If you wish to visit the tea shop at the beginning or end of your walk, start in Singleton where there is limited street parking. The tea shop is on the main road by the village pond. You will then start the walk at point 8.

THE WALK

1. Return to the road and turn right for 250 yards. A welcome footway starts at Cucumber Farm.

2. Immediately before a 'Singleton' sign, turn left on a signed bridleway. The track leads up to a gate. Through the gate, it becomes less distinct. Go ahead to a finger post then bear slightly left on a faint path to another finger post, indicating a cross path. Continue on to a gate, then ahead with a fence on the left to eventually arrive at another gate.

This is Levin Down Nature Reserve. The steep scarp slope of the South Downs faces north and the gentler dip slope faces south. The warm and sunny south-facing slopes have largely been ploughed up. Levin Down is an outlier of the main mass of the Downs and the south slope is too steep to plough so it is one of the few areas of chalk grassland with a southerly aspect. In fact, the name is thought to come from the Old English for Leave Alone Hill. It has a wonderful collection of chalk plants, such as the rich violet clustered bellflower and blue round-headed rampion, seen to best advantage when they are in flower in summer. The decline in grazing in recent

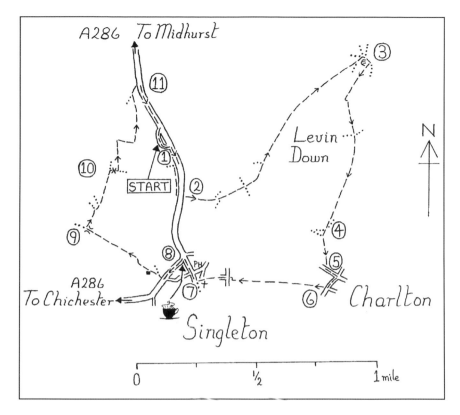

years has allowed scrub to invade including many juniper bushes. These are easy to recognise because the berries smell of gin! The vegetation supports a varied population of butterflies, including the Duke of Burgundy fritillary and the distinctive chalkhill blue. Levin Down is owned by the Goodwood estate and managed by the Sussex Wildlife Trust. As explained elsewhere (see walk 14), the wonderful springy turf of the Downs is a semi-natural habitat maintained by grazing and left entirely to itself it would revert to scrub and then woodland. Some scrub has been cleared and a flock of South Down sheep introduced. The management plan is to maintain a range of habitats and so the maximum diversity of species. Therefore, not all the scrub has been cleared. For example, the Duke of Burgundy fritillary, a brown and orange butterfly with a wing span of about an inch, is found along wood edges and in half shade.

3. Through the gate follow a track for 50 yards as it bears round to the right. Immediately after the entrance to a small, disused quarry, turn right on a signed path up steps to a stile. Then walk by a fence

15

on the left to a stile on the left into a wood. Follow the path through the wood and scrub along the hillside to meet a cross path in front of a fence.

The South Downs are made of chalk laid down at the bottom of the sea aeons ago and then thrown up into folds as a result of movements in the Earth's crust. During the last Ice Age they were not buried under ice but were an area of tundra, like Alaska is today. During this time, a thin layer of more acidic soil called loess was deposited on top of the chalk. This chalk heath supports more acid loving plants, such as heather, growing alongside chalk loving plants.

4. Turn right. After 25 yards fork left to remain by the fence to a stile, then press on across a field to a lane.

5. Turn left. At cross roads turn right, signed 'Goodwood 1', for 100 yards.

This is Charlton, once famous among the hunting fraternity. During the 18th century, the Charlton Hunt was the most famous in England. Its longest recorded chase started at 8 o'clock on the morning of 26th January 1738 and finished with a kill in Arundel Park at 6 o'clock, only three members having the stamina to stay the course to the end. The name of the pub, the Fox Goes Free, has a footnote in English social history. The Women's Institute was founded in Canada in 1897 and the first English branch (Singleton and East Dean) was launched here on 9th November 1915.

6. Turn right on a path signed 'Singleton 0.7m'. Posts show the line of the path as it heads for Singleton church, seen ahead. Go through a wooden kissing gate and follow the path between gardens to a road. Go ahead and when the road shortly ends, walk through an arch to the left of 4 Church Way. Follow the path past the church on the left to the entrance to Manor Farm on the left.

7. Turn right. Cross a road by the Fox and Hounds to the tea shop on the left.

Singleton is an attractive village of flint and brick buildings on the London Chichester road in the valley of the river Lavant. This is a 'winter bourne'; a stream that only flows when the water table in the underlying chalk is high enough, usually during the winter. In the tea shop are some photographs showing what can happen when the water table is really high! Parts of the church date back to Saxon times, when the manor, one of the largest and wealthiest in England, was owned by Earl

Godwin, father of the ill-fated King Harold, killed at the Battle of Hastings (see walk 18). The name lives on. Much of the surrounding area is owned by the Goodwood estate, Goodwood being a corruption of Godwin's wood. You may have noticed the tops of the grandstands at the racecourse visible above the Downs across the valley during the walk. Goodwood racecourse opened in 1801. In the days before modern transport, people had to stay locally during the races and Singleton was very crowded. There were bitter complaints from local residents about the rowdy behaviour and less savoury goings on among the racegoers and hangers-on.

8. From the tea shop turn left along the main road. Immediately past the post office on the right, turn right on a signed path. Go through a gate onto a cricket pitch. Skirt behind the club house to a stile by a gate, then walk along the right-hand side of a small field to a stile on the right. Over the stile, go ahead to a second stile onto a hedged path and follow this.

9. Immediately after crossing a brick bridge over a disused railway, do not go up steps ahead but turn right to a stile. Over the stile, press on to meet a track and turn right along it. At a junction with a second track after 40 yards, bear right.

This railway line opened in 1880. A station was built to serve the racecourse and it was a fine affair with a stained glass window and carpet in the waiting room. It closed to passengers in 1935 and goods traffic in 1954.

10. At the bottom of a dip, turn right under a bridge. After 20 yards cross a stile by a gate on the left. Head up the left-hand side of a field. At the top of the field, turn right to skirt round a wood on the left to eventually reach a stile. Over the stile go ahead to join a track and bear right to a road

Across the road is the entrance to 'Drovers', a fine 18th century house and once an inn with secret passages and cellars frequented by smugglers. It was bought by a member of the Egremont family of Petworth House (see walk 3) who converted it into a country house. Until then the road used to run beneath the windows but it was diverted away to maintain the family's privacy. The smugglers were brutal and vicious men (see walk 13). The Duke of Richmond, owner of the Goodwood estate, was not intimidated and several were hanged on the gallows on the Trundle on the other side of the valley. The gallows stood until 1791 when struck by lightning.

11. Turn right, back to the start.

Walk 3
PETWORTH

In the 18th century the Agricultural Revolution irrevocably changed the English landscape. The fields created by the Inclosure Movement were widely thought fussy and unattractive so the rich hired landscape gardeners to create an idealised version of what was fast disappearing. Only in recent times have these grand visions of a sweeping open landscape dressed with fine trees reached triumphant maturity – and nowhere more so than at Petworth Park, explored on this exceptionally attractive short walk. At the gates to the park is the ancient small town of Petworth, complete with a charming traditional tea shop. Petworth has enjoyed a long history as a market and estate town and is now a noted centre of the antiques trade with over 25 shops. If you enjoy beautiful landscape and poking about the back lanes and antiques shops of an old town, this walk should be top of your list.

☕ Tudor Cottage, Sadlers Row is a charming traditional tea room, complete with exposed beams. If you are tall, you will certainly have to watch your head! A full breakfast is served all day, except at lunchtime! Light meals include Welsh rarebit or omelettes, a selection of sandwiches and ploughman's. Full meals at lunchtime include roast of the day and daily specials. For tea a range of delicious cakes is offered including Sussex honeybread. Set teas include crumpet tea and clotted cream teas with extra clotted cream available. There is a choice of speciality teas including Earl Grey and Lapsang Souchong as well as herbal teas. They are open between 9 am and 5 pm from Monday to Saturday, opening at 10 am on Sunday, throughout the year, just closing between Christmas and New Year. Telephone: 01798 342125.

DISTANCE: 4 miles.

MAP: OS Landranger 197 Chichester and the South Downs or Explorer 133 Haslemere and Petersfield.

STARTING POINT: Petworth Park car park (GR 966238).

HOW TO GET THERE: Petworth Park car park is on the A283, Guildford-Petworth road, 1½ miles north of Petworth.

ALTERNATIVE STARTING POINT: If you wish to visit the tea shop at the beginning or end of your walk, start in Petworth. There is a car park in the middle of the town but I suggest using the one at the edge of the town on the A272 to Midhurst. Turn right out of the car park to pick up the walk at point 4.

THE WALK

1. Take a path from the rear of the car park, almost opposite the entrance. Follow this sometimes faint path as it descends into a small valley with a fine stand of mainly mature oaks on the right. Climb up the other side, as far as a lodge on the right, to find a cross track.

Petworth Park was designed by Capability Brown, who worked here from 1751 to 1764, and it is one of the finest examples of his work. As was his way, he carried out massive works, creating an idealised landscape. It is said that he shifted 47,000 tons of soil to create the lake, which is lined with 17,000 tons of clay – and all this in the days before the JCB was thought of! A herd of deer roams the park. They are fallow deer, not a native species. The Romans introduced some to this country but the ones in Petworth Park are thought to be of Eastern European origin and were imported into the Park in the 18th century. The estate and house were given to the National Trust in 1947 by the 3rd Lord Leconfield, whose ancestors, bearing one title or another, have been here since the 12th century.

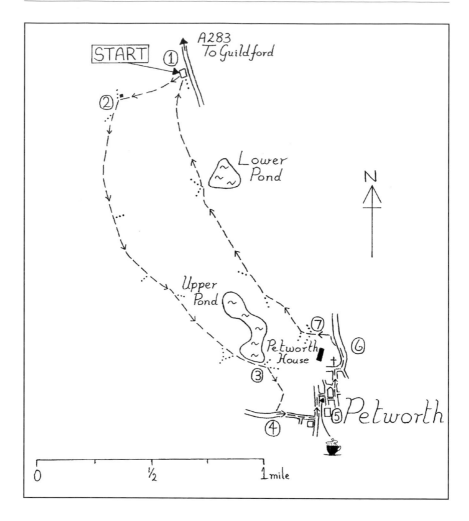

2. Turn left for about a mile. When a track joins from the right, continue ahead to the right of a small lake.

3. Some 40 yards after the end of the lake bear right on a grassy path that leads to a gate in a deer fence round a cricket ground. Cross the cricket ground to a gate in a wall giving onto a road.

4. Turn left into Petworth. At a mini-roundabout turn left. Take the first street on the right to the tea shop on the right.

Petworth is a fascinating little town and it is well worth taking the time to explore its quaint, twisting streets, packed with buildings that testify to the town's prosperity down the centuries. It has adapted to the modern world by becoming a centre of the antiques trade with over 25 traders.

5. Take the lane opposite the tea shop, Damers Bridge. At the end turn left up into Market Square. Leave the square by a cobbled street at the top right hand corner, Lombard Street. At the top, opposite a church, turn right then left on the A283, signed 'Guildford 19'.

Note the elaborate street lamp on the right, designed by Sir Charles Barry. It was erected by the town in 1851 as a token of their gratitude to Lord Leconfield for providing the town with gas lighting.

6. Turn left into The Cowyard entrance to Petworth Park. Walk between buildings to a tunnel on the left that leads beneath the formal gardens and into the park.

Petworth House dates from the end of the 17th century, and only the chapel remains of the earlier medieval manor. It is more a palace than a home with a succession of rooms stuffed with art treasures. George O'Brien Wyndham, the 3rd Earl of Egremont, lived at Petworth House from 1763 until 1837. A great patron of the arts, he bought works by over 60 notable artists and provided Turner with a studio to paint several studies of the park. He was also an agricultural innovator who experimented with cattle and pig breeding on his model farms and invested in roads and canals to move the produce. He allowed the title to die out, not marrying 'Mrs Wyndham' until their six children had been born. Petworth House is now in the care of the National Trust and is open from the beginning of April until the end of October, Saturday to Wednesday, between 1pm and 5.30pm. Telephone: 01798 342207. It deserves several visits to properly appreciate its treasures without becoming sated.

7. Follow a grassy path more or less straight ahead, up a knoll crowned with trees. At the top bear right as a path joins from the left and press ahead on a sometimes faint path. Follow the main path to the right of a second knoll. Ignore branches to the left by a small lake and continue on the path as it eventually curves right back to the car park where this walk started.

Walk 4
ARUNDEL

This walk packs more interest and variety into its 4 miles than many longer routes. Arundel Castle sits on a finger of high ground extending from the Downs to the river Arun with the ancient town huddling at its foot. The walk starts in the town, with its many interesting nooks and crannies, before entering Arundel Park. This is a beautiful stretch of the walk with outstanding views and ends beside Swanbourne Lake, overlooked by a tea shop. After tea the return to Arundel is a level stroll beside the river with unrivalled views of the town, castle and cathedral.

 Swanbourne Lodge is attractively housed in a building erected to guard one entrance to Arundel Park. As well as the attractive interior, there are tables outside overlooking the lake. A selection of cakes is offered and other teatime treats include cream teas and tasty Danish pastries. Lunches range from filled baguettes with both hot and cold fillings, through salads and ploughman's to full meals, including a roast. The desserts include a seasonal fruit pie. There is also a children's menu with attractions such as banana or peanut butter sandwiches. Swanbourne Lodge is open Monday to Thursday between 10.30 am and 5 pm and Sunday between 10.30 am and 6 pm throughout the year. Telephone: 01903 884293.

DISTANCE: 4 miles.

MAP: OS Landranger 197 Chichester and the South Downs or Explorer 121 Arundel and Pulborough.

STARTING POINT: Mill Road car park, Arundel (charge). (GR 020071). If this is full, there are other signed car parks in Arundel. Please note that some of this walk is within Arundel Park to which there is unrestricted public access on foot. However, dogs are not allowed.

HOW TO GET THERE: There are two exits for Arundel from the A27. Take the eastern one, signed 'Arundel Town Centre'. Immediately across a bridge over the river, turn right into Mill Road to a car park on the right opposite the entrance to Arundel Castle.

ALTERNATIVE STARTING POINT: If you wish to visit the tea shop at the beginning or end of your walk, continue along Mill Road to the tea shop to find some lay-bys on the right-hand side of the road. You will then start the walk at point 7.

THE WALK

The entrance to Arundel Castle is across the road from the car park. One of William the Conqueror's most favoured knights, Roger de Montgomery, first built a castle in about 1070 on the high ground overlooking the strategically important crossing of the river Arun. This first castle was probably a simple earth motte and bailey defended by a wooden palisade but by the 12th century this had been replaced by a formidable stone fortress, of which only the barbican and shell keep remain today. The castle has been besieged three times; in 1102 by Henry I, in 1139 by Stephen and by Parliamentary forces in 1643. In the Civil War siege the Parliamentary troops pounded it from a cannon mounted at the nearby church of St Nicholas, passed later on the walk. The present structure mainly dates from the rebuilding carried out at the end of the 18th century and then again at the end of the 19th century and so it is not the medieval fortification it seems but a relatively modern reproduction! However, this does not detract from its magnificence.

About 1800 one of the Dukes of Norfolk, owners of the Castle since the 16th century, introduced a colony of North American owls into the keep. Apparently, the birds were called after friends and relations with scant regard for gender so the

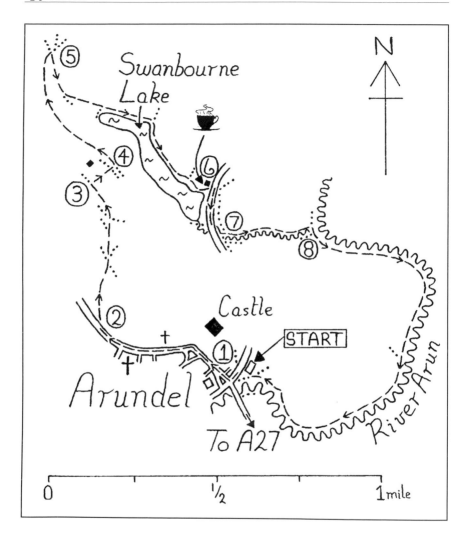

butler once announced, 'Please, your grace, Lord Thurlow has laid an egg.' This eminent bird died in 1859, aged over a hundred and the remaining owls had died out by 1870.

The castle is open from the beginning of April to the last Friday in October every day except Saturday between noon and 5pm. Telephone: 01903 883136.

1. Turn left out of the car park. Opposite the bridge on the left, turn right up the High Street, shortly with the castle walls on the right. At the top, follow the castle walls round to the left and continue ahead along London Road, signed 'London Dorking'.

Arundel has a wealth of interesting buildings and nooks and crannies too numerous to describe here. It is well worth taking the time to explore and an excellent pamphlet to guide you round is available from the Tourist Information Centre on the left as you walk up the High Street.

The line of London Road was changed in 1803 when the wall round the estate was built. The sign of the ancient St Mary's Gate Inn shows the old town gate, which now stands within the castle grounds. The road passes the ancient church of St Nicholas. It is a unique building as one end has the Catholic chapel with the tombs of the Fitzalan family while the other is the Anglican parish church. There is a wealth of interesting information available within. A little further along the road is the Catholic cathedral on the left. The Dukes of Norfolk have remained staunchly Roman Catholic despite past religious persecution, especially in the 16th century. Philip Howard, the 5th Duke of Norfolk, spent 11 years as a prisoner in the Tower during the reign of Elizabeth I and died there in 1595. He was canonised in 1970 and now the cathedral is partly dedicated to him. It was built by the 15th Duke between 1868 and 1873 and designed by Joseph Hansom, inventor of the safety cab named after him. It is a dominating building and was intended to be even more so as the original design included a 280 foot spire. This was never built because it was decided that the structure could not bear the weight.

2. Immediately after the entrance to Arundel Castle Estate Office, bear right on a surfaced drive to the Park Lodge entrance to Arundel Park and continue on the drive through the park, bearing right when the drive forks.

The drive passes the cricket ground where touring sides traditionally play their first match against the Duchess of Norfolk's XI.

3. As the drive approaches a turreted folly, turn right off the drive on a path across a grassy expanse. The point where the path leaves the drive is not visible on the ground but is marked by a yellow arrow on a post. Cross a gallop – a wide track surfaced with bark – and continue ahead and down a few yards to meet a cross track.

The folly is called Hiorne Tower. The architect Francis Hiorne built it in 1787 in the hope that he would win the contract to rebuild the castle. Sadly, he died two years later at the young age of 45.

4. Turn left along the track, over a stile by a gate, and follow the track down to a cross track in the valley below.

5. Turn sharp right. Follow the track for about a mile, shortly by Swanbourne Lake, to the tea shop on the left at the entrance to the park.

Swanbourne Lake is mentioned in the Domesday Book, when it was a millpond. It is fed by springs. The aquifer that feeds the springs is also used to supply Bognor and Littlehampton. This abstraction lowers the water table and so threatens the future of the springs and the lake. The management of the aquifer is the subject of research to protect its future. There is usually a wide variety of birds to be seen, visiting from the nearby Wetlands and Wildfowl Trust reserve.

6. Go through the entrance gate onto a road. Turn right for 250 yards.

7. At the conical turret of a bridge, turn left on a signed path. Do not go over a footbridge but take a path ahead along the left bank of a stream to the river Arun.

8. Turn right along the riverbank and follow it back to the car park.

The view of Arundel as you walk along the path beside the river is one of the best with the castle and cathedral above the town. The town grew up where the main east/west route crossed the river Arun. In those days, Arundel was a port with wharves along the river. There have been several suggestions about the origin of the name. The most obvious is that it means 'dell on the Arun'. An alternative is that it comes from 'Harhun dell', meaning the valley of horehound, a medicinal plant. More fanciful is that it is from the French 'hirondelle', meaning swallow, because it is the first place where summer reaches Sussex. Better yet it is named after the steed Hirondelle that carried the legendary Bevis of Southampton, one-time warder of the gatehouse of the castle. He was the original Desperate Dan who ate an ox a week with bread and mustard, washed down with two hogsheads of beer. When he felt death was near he flung his mighty sword from the tower and asked to be buried where it fell. A prehistoric grave in Arundel Park is known as Bevis's Grave.

Walk 5
AMBERLEY

This immensely varied route has all the elements that make walking in Sussex such a pleasure. It starts in a picture postcard village and climbs the Downs for an exhilarating ridge walk before a gentle descent to the river Arun. There are splendid views all around that amply reward the effort expended in climbing the 620 feet of Rackham Hill. A short walk by the river brings you to Houghton Bridge Tea Gardens. The final leg continues by the river and across flower-filled water meadows back to Amberley, passing beneath the walls of Amberley Castle.

 Houghton Bridge Tea Gardens overlook the river Arun. Where once wharves loaded commercial boats with chalk and lime and discharged coal to fire the furnaces, today the tables and chairs are positioned to watch the pleasure craft. There are boats for hire and trips on the Arun, if you wish to combine your walk with a jaunt on the river. There is also an indoor tea

room for less clement weather and you are asked to remove muddy boots
before entering. There is a selection of cakes or scones with cream. Lunches
range from sandwiches through filled jacket potatoes and ploughman's to
full meals, including a daily special. The many notices in the Tea Garden
servery may amuse you. They are open between 10.30 am and 5 pm every
day, extending to 5.30 pm at the weekends, between the beginning of April
and the end of October. Telephone: 01798 831558.

When the tea shop is closed, the Bridge Inn across the road, serves food.

DISTANCE: 7 miles.

MAP: OS Landranger 197 Chichester and the South Downs or Explorer 121
Arundel and Pulborough.

STARTING POINT: St Michael's church, Amberley (GR 028131).

HOW TO GET THERE: From the B2139 at Amberley take a lane into the main
part of the village, which lies north of the road. Take the first lane on the
left to the church. Some parking is available by the church hall, for
which a donation is requested. Should this be full, there is also limited
parking beyond the church beneath the walls of the castle, or other
spots round the village may be found.

ALTERNATIVE STARTING POINT: It is not easy to visit the tea shop at the
beginning or end of your walk. The car park at the tea shop is small and
patrons are asked not to leave cars for extended periods. Roadside
parking in the locality is very limited.

THE WALK

*Amberley is a delightful village of buildings dating from many centuries. Set
beneath the steep scarp slope of the South Downs above the flood plain of the river
Arun, the name is said to mean 'fields yellow with buttercups'. Its history goes back
to at least the 7th century, when King Cedwalla granted lands here to St Wilfrid.
There was certainly a Saxon church here and the present building dates from about
1100. Here too there are features from many times in the village's long history, from
wall paintings of the 13th century to a 20th century altar. There is more
information available within.*

1. Return through the village to the main road, the B2139.

2. Take Mill Lane opposite.

3. Bear left along the South Downs way when a lane joins from the
right. Some 100 yards after the junction turn left on a rough track
uphill, signed 'South Downs Way'. Follow this uphill, shortly

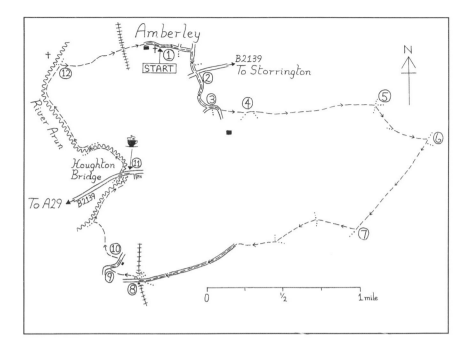

between fences, to a junction with a larger track leading from a farm on the right.

4. Turn left. After 70 yards bear left on a smaller track to continue climbing. Follow this track for about a mile to a cross path.

5. Turn right. The correct path leads along the right hand side of a field with a wood on the right, not a smaller path by a wire fence.

6. At a cross track turn right for about 3/4 mile. Ignore a path on the right after about a 1/4 mile.

7. At a track junction turn right. Ignore tracks right and left and continue when the track becomes a surfaced lane.

8. Watch on the left for a small windowless hut painted grey with a tall aerial and surrounded by a fence. You are above the railway, which goes through a tunnel. At this point, bear right on a track down to a cross track. Turn left for 10 yards then right on a signed bridleway. At the time of writing, the sign is very overgrown. This leads to a lane.

9. Turn right.

10. Some 25 yards after cottages on the right, turn left on a signed path that leads to a river bank. Turn right along an embankment to a road. Turn right to the tea shop on the left.

Once the air here was polluted with the acrid fumes produced by lime burning. Across the road chalk was gouged from the hillside. Wharves once operated where the tea shop now stands. Chalk and lime, produced by burning chalk, were exported by river and coal brought in to fire the furnaces. Later, large quantities of chalk were needed for the production of Portland cement, produced by firing chalk and clay at a high temperature. The quarry is now occupied by a working museum of industrial history that also houses the workshops of a range of rural craftsmen. It is open from March to October. Telephone: 01798 831370.

11. Return to the road and turn right to return across the bridge. Turn right to continue along the embankment, now with the river on the right, as far as a footbridge over the river. Cross the bridge and continue on the other side.

These water meadows are called Amberley Wild Brooks. Managed as a nature reserve, they are a haven for wildlife. John Ireland captured the play of light over the streams and meadows in his impressionistic piano piece, Amberley Wild Brooks, composed in 1921.

12. Level with a church across the river, turn right away from the river and follow a path from stile to stile, crossing a railway, to beneath the walls of Amberley Castle. Continue ahead as the track becomes a lane back to the church where this walk started.

In the 14th century, life was not so peaceful in this corner of England, which was under threat from French raiders (see walk 20). The Bishop Rede of Chichester found it advisable to fortify his summer residence and defend it with curtain walls that rise sheer from the water meadows. Charles II is supposed to have spent a night here in October 1651. While he was fleeing to the coast and exile after the Battle of Worcester, his horse cast a shoe on the Downs above and he took refuge in the castle. The manor and castle ruins cannot be visited, as they are now a hotel and restaurant.

Walk 6
PULBOROUGH

This is a very easy short walk. It is a route that will particularly appeal to bird watchers as it lies mostly within Pulborough Brooks Nature Reserve, a site of national importance managed by the Royal Society for the Protection of Birds. The tea shop is at the interesting Visitor Centre. A nature trail has been laid out to allow you to visit the Reserve and the hides that have been constructed. This is about 2 miles long and you should allow an extra couple of hours if you wish to combine this with the walk. One unexpected feature of such a level walk is the good views across the low lying Pulborough Brooks to the South Downs rising beyond.

 Upperton's Barn Tea-Room at Pulborough Brooks Nature Reserve is housed in a converted barn with windows overlooking the reserve. There is a wide selection of cakes, temptingly displayed. Filled jacket potatoes and sandwiches are offered for a light lunch and for heartier appetites there is a daily special – Italian sausage pasta on the day I visited. As well as the attractive interior, there are some tables outside on a very sheltered patio. It is open every day between 10 am and 4.45 pm except Monday when it closes at 3 pm. Telephone: 01798 875851.

DISTANCE: 3¹/₂ miles.

MAP: OS Landranger 197 Chichester and the South Downs or Explorer 121 Arundel and Pulborough.

STARTING POINT: The lay-by at the Pulborough United Reformed church (GR 059185).

HOW TO GET THERE: The starting point is on the north side of the A283 just east of the centre of Pulborough.

ALTERNATIVE STARTING POINT: If you wish to visit the tea shop at the beginning or end of your walk, start at Pulborough Brooks Nature Reserve where there is ample parking in the car park. The tea shop is in the Visitor Centre. You will then start the walk at point 6.

THE WALK

The Romans came this way. They founded Pulborough to guard Stane Street, the arterial route from London to Chichester, where it crossed the river Arun. Despite its important position, it did not develop into a major town and remains a straggling village. The more modern part, where this walk starts, lies along the A283 while the old part clusters round Stane Street, now more prosaically the A29.

1. Facing the road turn right along the road and walk past Rivermead on the left and Rectory Lane on the right to where Rivermead rejoins the main road.

2. Turn left along Rivermead. Turn right on a signed path between numbers 21 and 22. The path forks immediately after crossing a drainage ditch. Take the right fork, signed as a public footpath. Cross the river Chilt, a tributary of the river Arun, at a footbridge and walk on the left bank of the river Arun to a double stile. Continue by the river for a further 200 yards.

3. Turn left on a signed path away from the river. When the drainage ditch on the right bends right, go ahead to a stile by a metal field gate, not on the obvious path bearing right. Follow this path up to a cross path, then go ahead 10 yards to a stile beside a field gate.

4. Over the stile strike diagonally left to the far corner of a field to

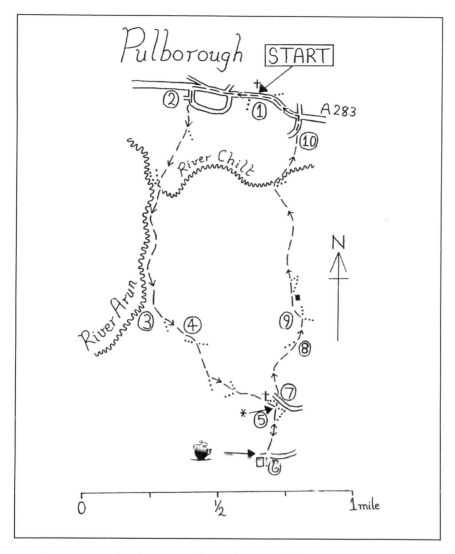

another gate and stile. Over this stile turn left on a signed path that soon becomes a track.

5. Just after passing a church on the left, watch for a fenced path on the right. Note this point and turn right along the path. (Note: the right of way leaves the track 50 yards further on and joins this path after 100 yards. The right of way is just about passable at the time of writing but for practical purposes has been replaced by the fenced path.) Follow the path to a car park. Turn right to the tea shop in the Visitor Centre.

Pulborough Brooks Nature Reserve was founded in 1989 when the RSPB bought the site as abandoned farmland. Water meadows are a threatened habitat because so many have been drained with the intensification of agriculture in the last 50 years. They are important for many birds and other wildlife and the RSPB has worked hard to produce a mosaic of habitats to conserve a diversity of species. Though the RSPB is primarily interested in birds, protecting and managing the whole ecosystem conserves these as well. There is therefore a profusion of other wild life, including many water meadow flowers. One important tool is controlled grazing, which is managed to give a range of grass heights. Some bird species, such as snipe, nest in the cover of long grass and feed on the soft, damp soil by pools and ditches. Others, such as lapwings, nest and feed on short grass where they can keep a look out for predators. In the winter the meadows are allowed to flood and this is now one of the most significant areas for over-wintering birds. As well as the Visitor Centre, with its welcome tea shop, there is a 2-mile nature trail that takes you round the reserve so you can learn more.

6. From the tea shop turn left and take the path on the left to retrace your steps to the point noted earlier (* on map). Now go ahead a few yards to a stile onto a lane.

The tiny 12th century church is dwarfed by the adjacent rectory. It was built for the shepherds tending their flocks grazing the Brooks. Outside, on the south-west corner, is a mass dial. This is a stone with a hole to take a stick. There are scratches to act as a sundial and it was a primitive time piece to enable the priest to know when to say mass in the days before clocks.

7. Cross the lane and take a signed path opposite along the left hand side of three fields to a track. The first of these fields in particular is a carpet of buttercups in season.

8. Turn right.

9. At a junction with another track turn left on a signed path down three steps. Follow the clear path from stile to stile, ignoring branches to the right after a cottage. Cross a footbridge, again over the Chilt, and walk with the river on the right then bear left to a stile and on to a lane.

10. Turn right to a road. Turn left back to the start.

Walk 7
FINDON AND CISSBURY RING

The mighty earthwork of Cissbury Ring has been unused for most of two millennia but it still towers above homes in the valleys around. This route explores its ramparts and, above all, offers unparalleled views of the coast from the Isle of Wight to Beachy Head before returning round the base of the hill. Once the ascent is completed, and this is not very daunting, it is easy walking all the way.

The conservatory style tea room at Wyevale Garden Centre, Findon also has a sheltered outdoor patio. All day-time meals are provided for from an English breakfast, served up till 11 am through snacks and full lunches to cream teas. There is a selection of cakes as well as other sweet temptations such as fruit pie and ice cream sundaes. It is open from 9 am to 5.30 pm every day except Sunday when the opening hours are 10 am to 5 pm. Telephone: 01903 874111.

DISTANCE: 4 miles.

MAP: OS Landranger 198 Brighton and Lewes or Explorer 121 Arundel and Pulborough.

STARTING POINT: Cissbury Ring car park, Findon Valley (GR 129076).

HOW TO GET THERE: From the A24, Worthing to Horsham road, at the northern edge of the built-up area behind Worthing take a residential road, Mayfield Avenue, signed 'P Cissbury Ring'. Take the first left, Storrington Rise, to the car park.

ALTERNATIVE STARTING POINT: If you wish to visit the tea shop at the beginning or end of your walk, start at Wyevale Garden Centre, Findon where there is ample parking. The tea shop is inside the Garden Centre. You will then start the walk at point 11.

THE WALK

1. From the rear of the car park cut across an open area to a cross path and turn right between a hedge and a fence.

2. When the path forks, bear right up to a small wooden gate into a field. Head slightly left up the field to find a fence with a gate into Cissbury Ring. Cross the first rampart and ditch and go up steps to the second rampart.

This extensive hillfort dates from the late Iron Age, about 200 BC. The ditch outside the ramparts is over a mile around and encloses an area of 82 acres. The ramparts themselves still rise to 20 feet. Originally, there were two lines of ramparts and an outer ditch and this arrangement can still be seen in places. It has been estimated that well over 50,000 tons of soil and rock must have been shifted a considerable feat of engineering with Iron Age tools. There is no sign that it was ever besieged and during the long Roman peace it was allowed to revert to pasture. Towards the end of the Roman period, when Sussex was under threat from Saxon pirates, Cissbury Ring was re-fortified. A turf wall increased the height of the original ramparts and the ditch was widened. This seems to have been the work of the local civilian authorities as there is no sign of Roman military architecture in the modifications.

3. Turn right on a path on the rampart as far as steps down onto a cross path.

This was the main entrance to the fort. Beyond the entrance the ditch was crossed by a causeway, which may have been intended for wheeled vehicles.

4. Turn left along the cross path and follow a broad grassy path.

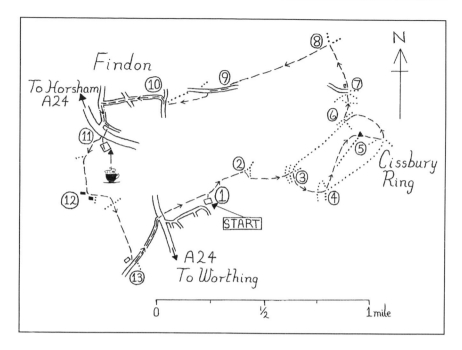

When this forks after a couple of hundred yards, bear left and follow it to a trig point.

This is the highest spot, at 602 feet, and has the best views: on a clear day you can see from Beachy Head in the east to the Isle of Wight in the west. During the Second World War, the South Downs were extensively used for military training. At this time, Worthing Museum received a skilfully carved chalk head, complete with a Hitler moustache, from an anonymous donor, with a note saying it had just been dug up at Cissbury Ring. So it had, but it had only been buried a short while before.

5. Facing the sea, bear left on a path that leads back to the ramparts. Turn left up some steps and along the ramparts.

The area around Cissbury Ring has many traces of flint mines sunk 2,000 to 4,000 years ago, long before the hillfort was built. Evidence of this important industry remains as grassy depressions. Flint tools from here have been found as far away as the eastern Mediterranean. Excavations in the 1950s found a tragedy from 4,000 years ago. The body of a girl was found lying where the roof of the mine had fallen in on her. She still held the remains of the torch she had to light her way.

37

6. Some 100 yards after a seat beneath a tree on the left, bear right off the ramparts down some steps and follow a stepped path down to a lane and a small car park.

7. Take a fenced track opposite to a cross path at the end of the first field.

From this distance you can better appreciate the scale of the ramparts of Cissbury Ring. Because they are referred to as hillforts, it is assumed they must have been primarily military but they were also gathering places and built to impress. The hillsides of forts were kept free of vegetation as a defensive measure with the result that the white chalk was visible. This must have been particularly impressive when the forts were in use, especially in sunshine or bright moonlight.

8. Turn left along the cross path to a lane.

9. Turn right for 150 yards then turn left to skirt round the left perimeter of a grassy area to a lane.

A market was held on Nepcote Green in the 13th century and it has been the site of a sheep fair since 1790. This is held on the second Saturday in September and includes the annual show of the Southdown Sheep Society as well as many other activities and attractions.

10. Take a lane almost opposite, Steep Lane. Continue ahead at a crossroads. Turn left at a T-junction to the A24 and a garden centre, with a tea shop, almost opposite.

11. Return across the car park and at the entrance turn left on a surfaced track. Continue along it until it ends at farm buildings.

12. Turn left in front of Stable Cottage on a clear track that eventually leads to a car park and lane.

A Saxon war chief, Aelle, landed at Selsey in AD 477 and settled in this area. He had three sons, one of whom was called Cissa. It is possible that both Chichester and Cissbury Ring were called after him. If he lived there, however, he left no trace.

13. Turn left along the lane. Cross the A24 and take a path opposite that leads back to the start.

Walk 8
DITCHLING BEACON AND STANMER

The ramparts of the scarp slope of the South Downs rise steeply from the Weald and there are many fine view points along the edge. Ditchling Beacon is one of the finest so be sure to choose a clear day to get the most from this exhilarating walk. Rather than the steep climb from the Weald, this route approaches from part way up the gentler dip slope behind. It uses a variety of downland, field and woodland paths, giving an unrivalled opportunity to study the interaction of man and landscape. The return visits Stanmer, an estate village tucked away in a fold in the Downs, and a good tea at the Village Stores should give you the energy to enjoy the short but steady climb back to the start.

Stanmer Village Stores has a tea room with some particularly delicious desserts, including outstanding fruit crumbles with custard, cream or ice-cream. Light lunches include things on toast such as Welsh rarebit, filled jacket potatoes and a good range of sandwiches. Other tea time temptations include cream teas and toasted crumpets. For a heartier appetite there is also an extensive selection of full meals. There are lots of tables outside. They are open every day from 9 am through into the evening. Telephone: 01273 604041.

DISTANCE: 6 miles.

MAP: OS Landranger 198 Brighton and Lewes or Explorer 122 South Downs Way, Steyning to Newhaven.

STARTING POINT: Upper Lodges car park, Ditchling Road (GR 324098).

HOW TO GET THERE: From the A27 Brighton by-pass, 2 miles east of its junction with the A23, take a minor road north signed 'Ditchling'. Turn left, again signed 'Ditchling', for a 1/4 mile to a car park on the right.

ALTERNATIVE STARTING POINT: If you wish to visit the tea shop at the beginning or end of your walk, start at Stanmer where there is ample parking in several car parks. The tea shop is in the village on the main street. You will then start the walk at point 8.

THE WALK

1. Take a surfaced track from the rear of the car park. Some 50 yards after passing lodges on both sides of the track, turn left on an unsurfaced track with a metal barrier. Immediately fork left. Ignore all further branches to the left and follow this pleasant woodland path to a stile into a field.

2. Cut across the corner to another stile then head initially along the right hand side of a field, following a clear path to a stile back into woods. Press on to a post, with the sign, 'This is High Park'. Bear left, signed 'Heathy Brow', to a road.

Note the dew pond on the right. Any rain that falls on chalk soon seeps into the permeable ground. Dew ponds were built to supply grazing animals. A depression was lined with clay to make a waterproof lining and it relies on rain – and dew – to maintain the pond.

3. Cross the road to a signed bridleway a few yards to the right. Follow this down the left-hand side of a field to a small metal gate. Immediately through the gate turn right and skirt round the top edge of the field to pick up a fenced path, signed 'Ditchling Beacon'. When the fences end, continue on the clear path.

4. At a T-junction with a cross path, turn right to Ditchling Beacon.

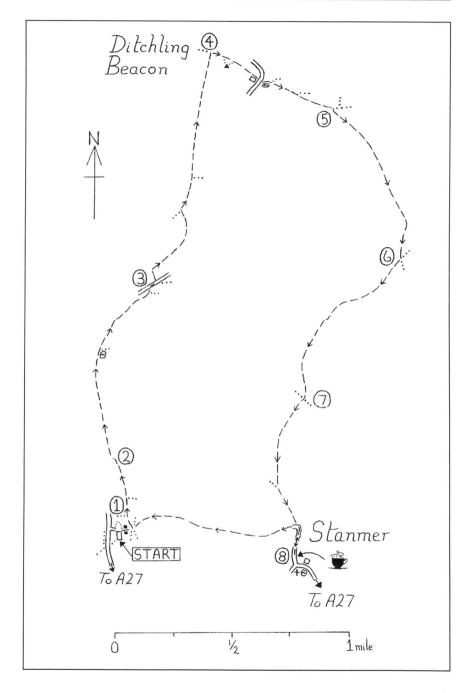

Ditchling
Beacon

N

START

To A27

Stanmer

To A27

0   ½   1 mile

Pass a car park and cross a lane, then continue along the edge of the slope with magnificent views to the left.

The 813 foot summit of Ditchling Beacon is the third highest point of the South Downs and one of the best viewpoints. On a clear day you can see right across the Weald to the North Downs. Once the site of a Neolithic hill fort (see walk 7), it was later used to carry an Admiralty fire beacon, which could be seen from Seaford to the North Downs. It was donated to the National Trust in memory of a young man killed in action during the Second World War.

5. At a clump of hawthorns turn right, indicated by blue arrows on a post, to find a small gate into a field. Bear diagonally right across the field down to a small gate. Through the gate, continue along the path down into a small valley and part way up the other side.

6. Some 175 yards after passing through a gate across the path, turn right through a wooden gate and follow the path down into a valley and along the bottom. Press on as the path enters woodland and climbs out of the valley again. The valley to the left of the wood delights in the name Moon's Bottom.

7. At the top go over a cross track and continue ahead, now downhill with Stanmer visible in the trees below. In Stanmer continue ahead through the village to the tea shop on the left.

Stanmer was the estate village for Stanmer House, built by the Pelham family in the 18th century. This has recently been restored and at the time of writing is about to be opened to the public. The village has all the elements – pretty cottages, a church and, of course, a tea shop! Brighton Corporation acquired Stanmer Park and the University of Sussex occupies part of it. This probably saved this lovely spot from the urban sprawl of Brighton and it is now managed for nature conservation and recreation.

8. Turn right from the tea shop to retrace your route through the village and follow the lane round to the left. Continue through the gate and follow the surfaced track back to the start.

Walk 9
ARDINGLY AND BALCOMBE

Ardingly and Balcombe are two attractive villages that face each other across a wooded valley bisected by a finger of higher ground. The valley has been flooded to make a Y-shaped reservoir, which has now blended with the landscape. This walk visits both villages and explores the valley between. It is a most pleasing expedition, with much of the route through woods and beside water. As this part of the Weald has a crinkly landscape, this is by no means a level walk, but it is very rewarding and justifies a good tea at a charming village tea shop.

 Balcombe Tea Rooms have an excellent array of cakes, displayed to tempt even the jaded appetite – not you if you have walked 3½ miles to get here! Other tea time goodies include cream teas with clotted cream, toasted tea cakes or cinnamon toast. Light lunches are available including home-made soup, sandwiches with a good selection of fillings, salads or omelettes. Teas include Assam, Lapsang Souchong and Earl Grey as well as herbal and fruit teas or coffee in an individual cafetiere. In winter, hot chocolate with whipped cream and a flake proves most acceptable! The interior is fresh and attractive and there are also a couple of tables outside. They are open Tuesday to Saturday 10.30 am to 5 pm and Bank Holiday Mondays. Telephone: 01444 811777

When the tea shop is closed, the pub in Balcombe, the Half Moon, serves food.

DISTANCE: 6^1/$_2$ miles.

MAP: OS Landranger 187 Dorking, Reigate and Crawley or Explorer 135 Ashdown Forest.

STARTING POINT: The lay-by opposite St Peter's Church Centre, Ardingly (GR 341298).

HOW TO GET THERE: From the B2028 at Ardingly, 4 miles north of Haywards Heath, take Street Lane, signed 'St Peter's Church and School' to a lay-by on the right just before the church, opposite St Peter's Church Centre.

ALTERNATIVE STARTING POINT: If you wish to visit the tea shop at the beginning or end of your walk, start in Balcombe where there is some street parking possible. The tea shop is near the centre of the village. You will then start the walk at point 11. Note: The South of England Show takes place in June each year at Ardingly Show Ground. If you plan to do this walk while the show is on, you will avoid difficulties with parking and traffic congestion by starting in Balcombe.

THE WALK

1. Facing the road, turn right along the road for 100 yards, towards the church. Opposite Jordans Cottage, turn right on a signed path to a T-junction with a broad, surfaced track.

2. Turn left. After 60 yards bear right to walk with a wire fence on the right on a surfaced track round the perimeter of Ardingly Show Ground on the right. When the perimeter track bears right, at a point where there are gates across the track, leave the track to continue in the same direction on a signed path, shortly passing through a metal gate. Follow the fenced path to a surfaced cross track.

For three days in June, Ardingly Show Ground is the home of the region's leading agricultural event, the South of England Show. During the rest of the year it hosts a wide variety of events such as dog shows, show-jumping competitions and antiques fairs.

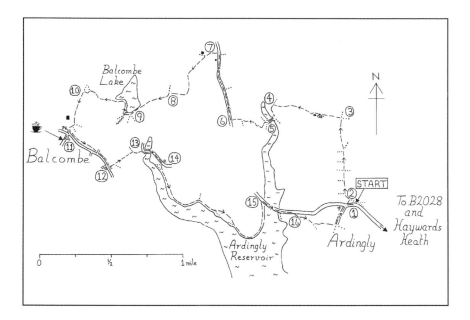

3. Turn left. Cross a stile beside a gate, then fork right to pass to the right of a pond. Go ahead to the right of farm buildings to a stile by a field gate. Head down the right-hand side of two fields, through a strip of wood and the right-hand side of a third field to a stile into woodland and a cross path.

4. Turn left. As the path bears left into Lodor Valley Nature Reserve, turn right across a long footbridge over an arm of a reservoir.

A tributary of the Sussex Ouse was dammed to form the 200 acre Ardingly reservoir, popular not only for its attractive setting but also for canoeing, sailing and trout fishing.

5. Over the bridge, turn right on a signed path. After 50 yards bear left at a fork and follow the path up through woods to a lane.

6. Turn right for about ½ mile.

7. Some 100 yards after North Lodge on the left, turn left on a signed path along the drive to Forest Farm. When the drive bends right to the farm, go ahead over a stile by a gate and walk down the left-hand side of a field to a stile. Over the stile, bear left to a stile by a gate into a field. (Do not mistake a gate on the left into a wood for this.) Over this stile turn right along the top of a field to a concrete farm track.

8. Turn left and follow the track past Balcombe Lake.

9. At the end of the lake, turn right over a stile by a gate on a signed path. Walk along the right-hand side of a field to a second stile and foot bridge. Over the footbridge, turn right to a stile into woods by the lake – an attractive spot to linger. Follow the main path through the wood, shown by occasional waymarks, to a T-junction with a signed cross path.

10. Turn left and follow the path out of the wood. Press ahead up a field past Balcombe House on the right to a track. Turn right into Balcombe. Cross Haywards Heath Road and go ahead to the tea shop on the right.

11. Return to the road junction and turn right. Walk out of the village, passing Mill Lane on the left.

12. Immediately before the next road on the left, Barn Meadow, turn left on a signed bridleway between a fence and hedge that leads to a gate into a field. Head across the field down to two gates. Go through the one on the right to follow a stepped path down through woods to a lane.

13. Turn right. Cross the reservoir and continue for about 250 yards to a small parking area on the left.

14. Turn right and follow a path down to and then beside the reservoir to eventually return to the lane.

Across the reservoir can be seen the imposing edifice of Ardingly College (pronounced Arding-lye). It was founded in the middle of the 19th century by the pioneering clergyman Nathaniel Woodard, along with Lancing College and Hurstpierpoint. Murray's Handbook for Travellers in Sussex, published in 1893, makes clear the social distinctions. Apparently, Lancing was 'for the education of the upper classes', Hurstpierpoint 'for sons of farmers', and Ardingly 'for sons of small traders'.

15. Turn right to cross another arm of the reservoir. Continue past the first path on the right and for a further 230 yards to the second path on the right.

16. Follow this narrow path through woods. When the path forks shortly after crossing a couple of foot bridges, bear left up through the wood. At the top of the hill, follow a path beside a fence to a lane. Turn left to the church then right to the start.

The Norman church was rebuilt in the middle of the 14th century and underwent substantial renovation in 1887 so it is a mixture of medieval and Victorian. The steps leading up to the tower are something of a puzzle. They are made of rough-hewn logs but why wasn't it continued down to floor level? At the other extreme of carpentry there is a fine 15th century screen. On the chancel floor are brasses to the Wakehursts and Culpeppers, who owned nearby Wakehurst Place. One shows a couple with ten sons and eight daughters. In 1643 the men of Ardingly used the church walls as a defensive position against Cromwell's dragoons, who had come to expel the Royalist rector.

Walk 10
CHAILEY COMMON

This walk passes a windmill at the traditional centre of Sussex. It stands near common land that is the last surviving fragment of lowland heath on the Low Weald and is designated a Site of Special Scientific Interest. The route explores the commons and some of the heavily wooded surrounding countryside, stopping off for tea at a charming traditional tea shop in North Chailey. The return is a pleasant stroll across more heathland.

May Cottage Tea Rooms is housed in a building that was once the village general store. An old photograph, taken in 1902, shows that teas were available then, though it has not been a tea room continuously since. It now sells antiques as well as serving teas and the walls are decorated with pictures by local artists. There are also a couple of tables outside. There is a most tempting selection of really delicious cakes and tasty sandwiches as well as daily specials at lunch time. It is open throughout the year except

January from Wednesday to Sunday between 10 am and 5 pm. Telephone: 01825 724150.

When the tea shop is closed, the King's Head in North Chailey serves food.

DISTANCE: 4 miles.

MAP: OS Landranger 198 Brighton and Lewes or Explorer 135 Ashdown Forest.

STARTING POINT: Red House car park (GR 392218).

HOW TO GET THERE: From the A275, East Grinstead to Lewes road, 1/4 mile north of its junction with the A272 at North Chailey, take a minor road west, signed 'New Heritage'. This is opposite the entrance to Grassington Farm. Red House car park is on the left after 1/4 mile.

ALTERNATIVE STARTING POINT: If you wish to visit the tea shop at the beginning or end of your walk, start in North Chailey where there is parking in lay-bys both sides of the road near the post office. The tea shop is at the crossroads, across the road from the King's Head and a garage. You will then start the walk at point 13.

THE WALK

Note: Chailey Common is a maze of footpaths. Please follow the directions carefully.

This is Chailey Common. Contrary to what many people believe, commons are not owned by the public. Common land is owned by someone but differs from ordinary land because some people other than the owner, the commoners, have rights over it. These are of various kinds; estovers is the right to pick up fallen timber for fuel and pannage is the right to graze pigs, for example. Chailey Common was recorded in the Domesday Book in 1086 and local people had grazing rights and also cut bracken and wood for fuel. These uses further impoverished an inherently poor soil and led to the establishment of the heath community we see today. Since the Second World War these rights are often not exercised because changes in farming practice make them uneconomic. This threatens the heath because gorse, birch and bracken can flourish, smothering the heather and grass. Chailey Common was declared a Local Nature Reserve in 1966 and has also been designated a Site of Special Scientific Interest. The management plan aims to control the invasion of scrub by mowing and controlled grazing. Sheep were introduced in 1991 to help in this control.

1. With your back to the road, leave the car park on a path on the right of the first parking area over a plank bridge. Ignore two paths

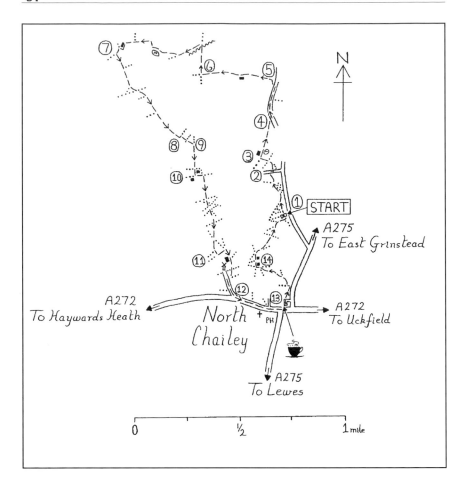

N

START

A275
To East Grinstead

A272
To Haywards Heath

A272
To Uckfield

North
Chailey

PH

A275
To Lewes

0   ½   1 mile

that fork left after 10 yards and go ahead to join a larger path coming in from the left. Fork left after 75 yards – the right fork leads to a lane and footpath sign. Follow the main path gently downhill to a major fork after 120 yards, ignoring minor paths forking right after 20 and 45 yards. Bear right to a surfaced farm drive.

Only the owner and those who have commoners' rights have automatic right of access to common land. The public only has the usual access on public rights of way. Abuse of commoners' rights and attempts to illegally remove those rights to develop the land led to many problems and so to simplify the position, all common land was registered under the Commons Act 1965. The local Parish Council now mainly owns Chailey Common and you are welcome to wander at will over the 450 acres, hence the maze of footpaths

2. Turn right for 25 yards then left on a track that shortly joins another drive coming in from the right. Follow this down to a T-junction with a tarmac drive.

3. Turn right, signed 'Broadwater House', passing between the house and a pond. Just before the drive ends at a turning circle, turn left on a less than obvious path that leads down through woods to emerge on a lane.

4. Turn left.

5. Bear left along a track to Rock Cottage and Lindfield Farm. Walk past cottages and farm buildings and continue along the track.

6. At a cross path turn right over a stile. Walk down the right-hand side of a field to a stile by a gate. Go ahead a few yards to a second stile and turn left, signed 'West Sussex Border path 1989'. Cross the bottom of a field to another stile and gate. Cross the next field but do not go into the one beyond. Turn right to walk up the edge of the field with a hedge on the left to a stile in the top left corner. Over the stile turn right, as shown by a finger post, to skirt the right perimeter. Ignore a path on the right and carry on round the field to a stile by a gate onto a track by farm buildings.

7. Turn left along the track for 30 yards then turn left on a signed path that leads down the left hand side of a field into a valley. Bear left and follow what is now a track out of the valley and on along the right-hand side of a field and over a causeway over a marshy area.

Ponds and lakes are always temporary features of the landscape. As time goes by they are filled in with sediment carried by the streams that flow into the lake and by the accumulation of the remains of the plants and animals that live there. The area of open water gradually gets less and less and is replaced by marsh. The marsh plants here include horsetails. These are living fossils, related to plants that thrived millions of years ago in the Carboniferous era, before the age of the dinosaurs, and whose remains formed most of the coal deposits in the Earth's crust. The horsetails can be recognised by their distinctive rings of leaf-like structures. In the past, they were collected and used to scour pots.

8. Immediately after emerging in a field turn left over a footbridge then right to carry on in the same direction, shortly crossing a track, to meet a cross path at the far end of the field.

9. Turn right over a stile and walk up the right hand side of a field and past barns to a track.

10. Turn left for 50 yards. At the entrance to Great Noven Farm turn right through two metal field gates next to a small wooden gate. Walk down the right-hand side of a field into a wooded valley and up the other side, crossing several paths and ignoring small branches left. You are now back on Chailey Common.

11. At the top of the hill bear left, then turn left at a T-junction with a cross path. Turn right on a cross path at a prominent post marked with yellow arrows. Pass a large building and windmill on the right. Cross a track and go ahead to a drive. Turn left to a main road.

Chailey Heritage on the right has a world-wide reputation for the education and rehabilitation of handicapped children. It was founded in 1903 as an offshoot of a London home for boys with tuberculosis called, in the fashion of the times, 'The Guild of Brave Poor Things'. With the decline of TB it expanded its work to deal with disabilities such as spina bifida and cerebral palsy.

The smock mill dates from about 1830 and is supposed to stand at the centre of Sussex. It may be visited on the last Sunday of each month from April to September between 3pm and 5pm.

☕ **12.** Turn left through North Chailey to the tea shop on the left at the cross-roads.

13. Leave the tea shop through the car park at the rear. Turn left along a lane and when this bends right carry on in the same direction on a path. At a track turn left then almost immediately right. This path initially continues in the same direction, parallel with the road, and then bears left away from the road and meanders across the common to a cottage with ivy-covered walls.

14. Turn right by the side of the cottage and walk past a second cottage. Bear right at a fork just past the end of the second cottage's garden. After 75 yards bear left at a second fork. This path leads back to the car park where the walk started.

Walk 11
ASHDOWN FOREST

Less than 40 miles from central London is the last untamed fragment of the mighty forest that once stretched from Hampshire to Kent and from North to South Downs. The Venerable Bede, writing in the 8th century, referred to it as, 'thick and inaccessible, a retreat for ... wolves and wild boars'. The animals are long gone but it is still a wild place. The backbone of Ashdown Forest is a sandstone ridge. This route starts with a climb to a view-point then an exhilarating walk along the ridge with tremendous views. After a visit to a restored windmill the route sweeps round off the ridge to a famous traditional tea shop for refreshment before completing this outstanding and highly recommended walk.

Duddleswell Tea Rooms is a charming, traditional establishment set in the heart of the Forest. It offers an excellent selection of cakes and other tea-time goodies including Marmite soldiers and crumpets with lashings of butter and strawberry jam. At lunchtime there is a blackboard with daily specials including, on my visit, a delicious vegetarian homity pie. Other lunch suggestions include salads and things on toast. Cream teas include Jersey cream and one or two scones, though having climbed the hill to get here, you can feel justified in indulging in two! There are plenty of tables outside and an undercover area outside is being developed. It is open throughout the year, except for four weeks in December and January, every day except Monday (open Bank Holiday Mondays) between 10 am and 5 pm from April until September, closing at 4.30 pm in the darker months. Telephone: 01825 712126.

There is no other source of refreshment on the walk.

DISTANCE: 5 miles.
MAP: OS Landranger 198 Brighton and Lewes or Explorer 135 Ashdown Forest.
STARTING POINT: Gorsey Down car park (GR 475286).
HOW TO GET THERE: From the B2026, Hartfield Uckfield road, about a mile south of its junction with the B2188, take a minor road east, signed 'Crowborough 3¾' for ¼ mile to a car park on the right at the track to Crest Farm.
ALTERNATIVE STARTING POINT: If you wish to visit the tea shop at the beginning or end of your walk, start in the car park opposite the tea shop in the hamlet of Duddleswell on the B2026. You will then start the walk at point 13.

THE WALK
Note: Ashdown Forest is freely open to walkers and is a maze of paths. Some are marked on the Ordnance Survey maps and some are more informal. Please take particular care following the directions.

1. With your back to the road, take a small path from the right rear of the car park. At a T-junction with a cross path turn right and follow it to the road.

2. Turn left to the main road.

The fence on the right surrounds a former Diplomatic Wireless Service Station where messages to and from embassies all over the world were transmitted and received. The station was opened in 1942 to broadcast anti-Nazi propaganda and remained in use until 1985. In 1988 it was reported in the local press that a large bunker was being constructed behind the fence to act as a seat of local government in the event of a nuclear attack.

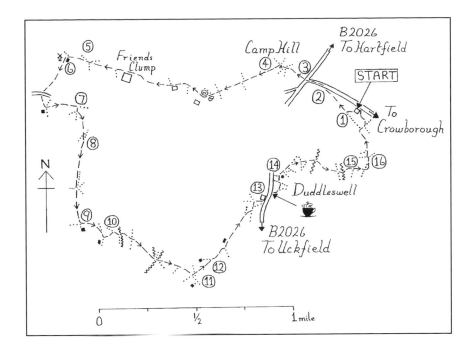

3. Cross the main road to a small gate then follow the path uphill to Camp Hill, crowned with a clump of pines. There are several seats here to admire the magnificent view.

Camp Hill gets its name from a huge army encampment set up here in 1793 during the French Wars. Detachments of 12 regiments were stationed here. A series of mounds north of Camp Hill long puzzled archaeologists who named them 'Mystery Mounds'. It has now been established that they are nothing more exciting than the remains of the camp kitchens!

4. Pass to the left of the clump then turn left on a broad crossing track. Follow this gently downhill, passing between attractive ponds. Do not go into the car park ahead. At the end of the pond on the right, bear round to the right to pass the car park on your left and continue ahead gently uphill to Friends Clump on the right and another car park on the left. Carry on ahead, now downhill.

The Romans named this area Sylva Anderida, to the Saxons it was Andreadswald and to medieval people it was The Weald, which means wood. The expanses of open heath are the result of centuries of deforestation. Some of the trees were deliberately cut down to make fuel and charcoal for the iron industry. Grazing also played its part as the nipping teeth of animals prevented new trees from growing to take the place of those that became old and died. This wild heath is a man-made landscape! William Cobbett visited it in 1822. He described '...verily the most villainously ugly spot I ever saw in England. This lasts you for five miles, getting, if possible, uglier and uglier all the way, till, at last, as if barren soil, nasty spewy gravel, heath and even that stunted, were not enough, you see some rising spots, which instead of trees present you with black, ragged, hideous rocks.' Not his favourite place, we may surmise! The clumps of conifers are of comparatively recent origin, many having been planted in the 19th century with the deliberate intention of enhancing the landscape.

5. Just after a fence starts on the left, bear left at a fork, signed 'Windmill'. Bear left again at another fork to go through a gate onto a track between a cottage and Nutley Windmill.

Nutley Windmill is the oldest working mill in Sussex. It was probably built in Crowborough about 1675 and moved to its present site in 1810. It was in use until 1908 and then lay abandoned and rotting until it was rescued by a dedicated band of enthusiasts. It is an unusual design (an open trestle post mill), one of only five survivors of this type in Britain. It has no fan tail and has to be pushed round to meet the wind. It is open to the public on the last Sunday of the month between 2.30pm until 5.30pm from June to September.

6. Turn left along the track to a road and continue on a signed path opposite. Cross a track leading past a modern house called 'Alma Cottage'.

7. At the bottom of a dip turn right, passing a wooden horse barrier and 'No Horses' sign. Some 30 yards after the barrier the path forks into three. Take the left branch to contour along the top of a valley then into woodland to shortly meet a more substantial cross path.

8. Turn right. You will soon notice a substantial track parallel with the path, which it eventually joins at a cross path. Carry on in the same direction along the track.

9. Just before the track reaches a building bear left along a track over a cattle grid. Some 20 yards before the track reaches Misbourne Farm, turn left on an unsigned path that soon meets a cross path.

10 Turn right. Follow the path down into a valley and steeply up the other side, over a cross track and down into another valley where two streams meet. Ignore tracks to right and left and carry on steeply out of the valley, ignoring a path on the right.

The water in the stream is usually a rusty colour due to the iron leached from the rock. Some 135 million years ago, this part of the earth's crust was a huge, freshwater lagoon. Rivers flowing into it carried sediments eroded from the surrounding land and these were deposited on the floor of the lagoon and eventually compressed into sandstone and clay. During this process of deposition, a series of chemical processes caused the iron to become concentrated. The iron-rich rock was mined and smelted since the Iron Age: the 16th and 17th centuries were the boom times when the Weald was providing much of Britain's iron. A source of carbon is an essential ingredient of the smelting process. Traditionally this was charcoal and the demand for this was one of the main reasons for the deforestation of Ashdown Forest. Charcoal supplies became difficult and eventually charcoal was replaced by coke, made from coal. The industry collapsed in the early 19th century in the face of competition from Scotland and the north of England. There is still a legacy in place names in the Forest, such as Boring Wheel Mill, Furnace Farm and Old Forge Lane.

11. At the top of the hill turn left on a cross path. (If you reach a track that leads to barns on the right, you have gone 80 yards too far.) Go over a made-up track, still climbing gently, to reach a second surfaced track leading from a house on the left.

12. Turn right. When the track bends sharp right continue ahead passing a house called 'Little Gassions'. Follow the path to a T-junction with a broad cross path, ignoring all paths on the left. Turn left to a surfaced drive. Turn right to a road then left to the tea shop on the right.

Not all the people in the forest's past were respectable farmers and iron workers. Its wild remoteness meant it was the ideal territory for poachers, horse thieves and smugglers. Duddleswell was a notorious haunt of smugglers, whose trains of packhorses came up by night from the coast along remote tracks, safe from the excisemen. It is said that during the 16th century they even smuggled cannon made from local iron out of England to the country's enemies.

13. From the tea shop take a track adjacent to the building for 60 yards then turn left on a grassy path leading to a track. Turn left for

15 yards then right on a narrow, unsigned path to a surfaced drive. Turn right in front of a house then continue ahead on an unsigned path.

14. Note where the holly hedge on the right ends. Go ahead for 35 yards, ignoring two immediate paths on the right opposite a field gate, to find a clear path on the right. Do **not** take this but continue for a further 15 yards to a small, grassy path that forks right. Take this one, gently downhill. Cross a larger path after 90 yards and carry on down to a plank footbridge over a stream. Press on up the other side. The path becomes rather obscure for a while as it twists through the trees: at the time of writing, it is marked by yellow arrows. It leads to a small gate into a field. Through the gate head slightly right to a stile onto a surfaced drive. Go straight over the drive to continue on the path. Cross a stream after 25 yards then bear left uphill to a track.

15. Turn left. This is the Weald Way. Continue along the track when the Way cuts out a pronounced left-hand bend and then rejoins the track 50 yards after the bend at a way-mark on the left.

The Weald Way cuts across the south-east corner of England from Gravesend to Eastbourne, a distance of 82 miles.

16. Some 50 yards further on there is a way-mark post on the right. At this point turn left and immediately bear right to a stile marked with the WW way-mark. Continue to a track. Turn right. At a T-junction of tracks, turn left back to the start.

Walk 12
HARTFIELD AND POOH BRIDGE

This is a walk with Pooh Bear and Christopher Robin, immortalised by A. A. Milne and the illustrator E. H. Shepard. It starts at Pooh car park and explores the northernmost tip of Ashdown Forest and the High Weald round Hartfield. The landscape the route covers is varied and outstanding. Some is through one of the largest woods remaining in Ashdown Forest and the rest across that most English of landscapes – flower-filled meadows thickly decorated with mature trees. The tea shop is in an attractive village – and there is honey for tea!

Stairs Farm House on the High Street in Hartfield is a lovely listed 17th century building with teas served indoors, in a conservatory or on a patio overlooking the garden. The menu features a cream tea or a Pooh Bear tea with honey. There is also a very tempting selection of cakes and puddings. For lunch there are tasty sandwiches, salads or filled jacket potatoes. A ploughman's is served with Sussex farmhouse cheese while a farmer's lunch has home baked gammon and a fisherman's lunch includes prawns, smoked salmon and smoked mackerel. They are open between 10.30 am and 5.30 pm in summer, closing at 4 pm in winter, every day except Tuesday. Tel: 01892 770793.

When the tea shop is closed, the pubs in the village serve food.

DISTANCE: 5^1/$_2$ miles.

MAP: OS Landranger 188 Maidstone and the Weald of Kent or Explorer 135 Ashdown Forest.

STARTING POINT: Pooh car park, Chuck Hatch (GR 473333).

HOW TO GET THERE: From the B2026, Hartfield to Uckfield road, 1^3/$_4$ miles south of Hartfield, take a minor road west at Chuck Hatch to Pooh car park on the right.

ALTERNATIVE STARTING POINT: If you wish to visit the tea shop at the beginning or end of your walk, start in Hartfield where there is some street parking. The tea shop is at the south end of the village on the main road. You will then start the walk at point 8.

THE WALK

1. Return to the lane and turn left and left again at the B2026, signed 'Hartfield 1^3/$_4$'.

2. Opposite a house called 'The Paddocks' turn right on a path marked by a stone sign. Follow the path down into a small valley and across a stream at a footbridge. Press on through the wood, ignoring two paths on the right. At the top of a short rise the Weald Way joins from the right. Continue ahead when the track becomes a surfaced drive leading to Kovocs Lodge.

Ashdown Forest is the largest area of south-east England that has never been under the plough. This is Five Hundred Acre Wood – one of the largest remaining woods. The word 'forest' did not originally mean an area covered with trees. It referred to a royal hunting area and that is precisely what Ashdown Forest used to be. Records from the 13th century show that this was a popular hunting area for royalty and noblemen and this is recalled by names such as Hindleap Warren and Kings Standing: a standing was a raised shooting box from which the hunters shot at deer driven past by keepers. By the end of the 13th century the Forest was enclosed by a pale. This consisted of a bank with a fence on top and a parallel ditch on the inside. This design made it easy for the deer to jump in and hard to jump out. As time passed, fashionable society lost interest in hunting, the Forest was neglected and by 1657 all the deer had gone. For the next 200 years there was a succession of legal

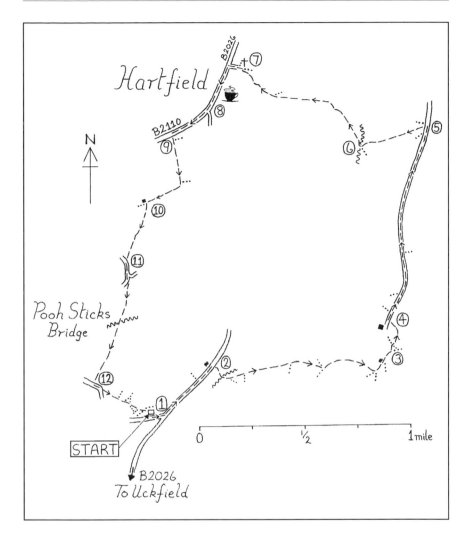

wrangles as would-be 'improvers' tried to develop the area and commoners resisted their efforts. Finally, in 1865 an Act of Parliament settled matters. Commoners' rights were recognised and the public given legal rights of access to specified areas, while other parts are in private ownership. Management of the Forest was given to an elected Board of Conservators whose duty is to preserve the Forest's unique character for all time. In 1988 the owners, the de la Ware family, sold it to East Sussex County Council and the freehold is vested in the Ashdown Forest Trust. (See also walk 11.)

3. Some 75 yards after passing an isolated cottage called 'Forest Place' bear left when the drive forks. After a further 40 yards cross another track and continue in the same direction on a path way-marked with the WW Weald Way sign. The path lies between fences where it has been diverted away from an imposing house and leads to a surfaced drive.

4. Turn right for about a mile.

This drive gives extensive views of the forest. This is a delightful part of the walk and the easy going means you can fully enjoy the views. Before long, Hartfield church spire comes into sight and you will be pleased to know that the tea shop lies just beyond.

5. Some 60 yards after a drive on the left to Old Buckhurst, and immediately before a second track, turn left over a stile to pick up a faint path that leads diagonally left to a second stile into a wood. Through the small wood, follow the faint path round to the right. Do not cross a rustic pole bridge on the right but continue for 40 yards and turn right through a metal field gate and cross a brick bridge over a stream.

6. Now walk up the right-hand side of a field. At the end go through a gate on the right and ahead to a second gate. Now bear diagonally left across a field then along the right-hand side of two further fields to a stile onto a track by a church.

7. Turn left into Hartfield. At a main road turn left to the tea shop on the left.

Though on the edge of the wildest area of south-east England, Hartfield is a very civilised place, which has won the Best Kept Village competition. On the right of the track into the village is the entrance to the church. The lychgate originally led into the churchyard under a pair of Tudor half-timbered cottages, but only one remains. A yew tree grows where its partner once stood.

8. From the tea shop turn left and walk out of the village on the B2110, signed 'Forest Row 4'.

A. A. Milne lived at Cotchford Farm, half a mile south of Hartfield. The adventures of the greedy bear and his companions all happened in the surrounding forest and the illustrations of E. H. Shepard were based on real locations. The landscape of Ashdown Forest lives in the childhood memories of all who were raised on the stories and perhaps that is one reason why it is so attractive to so many people. The shop specialising in 'Pooh-phernalia', passed on the right, is housed in a Queen Anne house and stocks all sorts of souvenirs.

9. Near the top of a hill turn left on a drive to Hook Farm House. When this bends left after a few yards, continue in the same direction on a signed path across two fields. In a third field ignore a signed path on the left and continue for 30 yards to a stile by a gate on the right. Over the stile, walk along the right-hand side of a field to a drive leading to a house.

10. Cross the drive to a stile onto a signed path that leads down into a valley to a lane.

11. Turn left. Bear right at a fork and continue in the same direction on a path when the lane bends right after 40 yards. This leads to Pooh Bridge. Cross the bridge and carry on along the path to a lane.

This is the bridge where Pooh and Christopher Robin played poohsticks. It was originally built in 1903 and has been recently restored. Many of the other locations, such as the North Pole, Roo's sand pit and the Enchanted Place are south of the area covered by this walk.

12. Turn left for 60 yards. As the lane swings right at the entrance to Andbell House, continue in the same direction on a path. Ignore all side paths and bear left at a major fork. Bear left at the next fork and take the right option immediately after a wooden horse barrier. This leads back to the car park where this route started.

Walk 13
LITLINGTON

Isolated and invisible to the motorists speeding by on the main Eastbourne to Seaford road a few hundred yards away, Westdean nestles in a hollow surrounded by ancient downland and new, man-made forest. The outward leg wends its way through Friston Forest via this ancient hamlet to Litlington, another delightful village with a number of chocolate-box cottages. The return leg is, unusually, slightly longer and is a very easy, level stroll by the Cuckmere River.

 The charms of this beautiful corner of Sussex were well known to previous generations and the Tea Gardens that are the focus of this walk have been in existence in this delightful spot for 150 years, making it the oldest such establishment in Sussex. The lawns are set with tables and chairs and for less clement weather there are some wooden pavilions giving undercover accommodation. They offer a range of set teas from a Sussex Cream Tea with scones and jam and cream as well as cake to an English Tea with cucumber sandwiches. There are delicious cakes. For a light lunch choose from salads, soup and sandwiches. Litlington Tea Gardens are open from the weekend before Easter to the last Sunday in October from 11 am until 5.30 pm. Telephone: 01323 870222.

When the Tea Gardens are closed, the pub in Litlington, the Plough and Harrow, serves food and there is also a restaurant at the Country Park car park where this walk starts.

DISTANCE: 4¹/₂ miles.

MAP: OS Landranger 199 Eastbourne and Hastings or Explorer 123 South Downs Way, Newhaven to Eastbourne.

STARTING POINT: Seven Sisters Country Park alternative car park (GR 518995).

HOW TO GET THERE: From the A259, Seaford to Eastbourne road, at Exceat take a minor road, signed 'Westdean ³/₄ Litlington 1³/₄' to the car park entrance on the right.

ALTERNATIVE STARTING POINT: If you wish to visit the tea shop at the beginning or end of your walk, there is a car park at the Tea Gardens but permission must be sought before leaving your car for a long period. The street parking in the village is very limited. You will then start the walk at point 6.

THE WALK

Friston Forest was acquired by the Forestry Commission in 1926 and now extends to 1,600 acres of native hardwoods, mainly beech, and quick growing conifers such as Scots and Corsican pine. The soil over the chalk of the Downs is thin and fierce, salt-laden winds can blow. The conifers were planted to protect the young broad-leaved trees and are gradually being removed to reveal a magnificent beech forest. Goldcrests, linnets, crossbills and nightingales all make their home in the forest.

1. Return towards the entrance to the car park and turn right on a public bridleway, signed 'Westdean', shortly passing two wooden sculptures erected to commemorate 25 years of successful Dutch elm disease control in East Sussex. Stay on the main track, ignoring a right fork 100 yards after passing the sculptures and all other turns left and right, to a major cross track at Westdean.

2. Turn left, signed 'South Downs Way Litlington'. Almost immediately cross a lane and walk up a lane opposite to the right of Forge Cottage. When the lane bends right, continue ahead on a track signed 'South Downs Way'. Bear right on a path at the entrance to 'The Glebe' and follow it uphill.

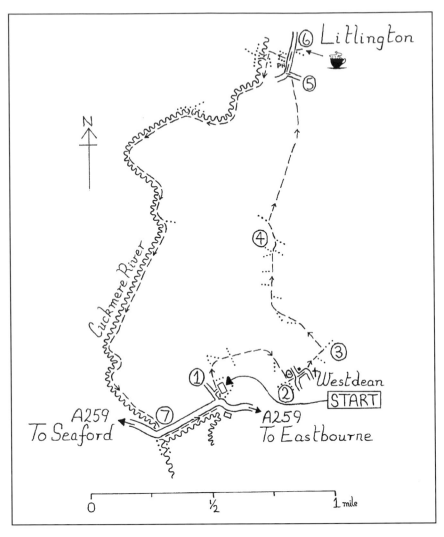

The tiny, hidden hamlet of Westdean has roots that are thrust deep into English history. Alfred the Great is said to have had a palace here. It is a peaceful place of high flint walls and huge barns. The church, to the right of the route, is partly Norman and worth a look, if you have time. Inside is a modern memorial bust by Epstein of the 1st Viscount Waverley, better known as Sir John Anderson, a member of Churchill's war cabinet, who lived and is buried here. The adjacent 14th century rectory has been much altered down the centuries and is one of the oldest inhabited houses in Sussex.

3. When the fence on the left ends, turn left, still following South Downs Way signs, and follow the path along the side of a valley then down to a T-junction with a cross path.

4. Turn left for 120 yards then cross a stile on the right. Follow the path up the left-hand side of two fields and the right-hand side of a third. In a fourth field bear slightly left downhill to a small gate onto a lane.

Look across the valley and you can see the outline of a white horse carved into the hill by a local farmer in the 19th century. During the Second World War it was covered over to prevent the Germans using it as a navigational aid.

5. Turn left, then right at a T-junction to the tea shop on the right.

6. Turn left out of the Tea Gardens and retrace your steps along the lane for 100 yards. Turn right on a surfaced path, signed 'Alfriston 1 mile' and follow this to a bridge over a river. Do not cross the bridge but take a path along the bank to walk with the river on the right, eventually to reach a road.

The river Cuckmere was too small to be commercially navigable so no castle was built to defend it and no major town developed. Its loneliness made it popular with smugglers and the flow of contraband up the Cuckmere valley was a major problem for the excisemen. Nowadays, we tend to romanticise smuggling: it inspired Rudyard Kipling, who lived for a while at nearby Rottingdean, to write his well-known poem:

> *'Five and twenty ponies trotting through the dark,*
> *Brandy for the parson, baccy for the clerk.'*

In fact, organised crime is rarely attractive in any century. At the beginning of the 19th century Cuckmere Haven was used by the Alfriston Gang. They lured an exciseman to his death on the cliffs by moving the blocks of stone marking the path. As he clung to the cliff and begged the smugglers to rescue him, they stamped on his fingers and he hurtled to his death. The leader of the Gang, one Stanton Collins, was eventually arrested and transported to Australia, not for smuggling but for sheep stealing.

7. Cross the road and turn left. At a junction recross the road and take a short path back to the car park.

Walk 14
WILMINGTON AND THE LONG MAN

Starting at the feet of the famous Long Man of Wilmington, this is an exceptionally varied and highly recommended walk. It starts with a climb round to his head followed by a walk along the top of the Downs with outstanding views. The descent could not be more different, using ancient, sunken tracks that lead to Folkington, a tiny Downland hamlet with a 13th century church. The route then leads round the bottom of the Downs by quiet field paths to a tea garden on the edge of Wilmington before a gentle stroll through the village back to the start.

 Wishing Well Tea Rooms are set in a delightful garden with a charming, airy pavilion. It is a friendly establishment with excellent service. They serve delicious cakes and other tea time favourites such as scones with cream or toasted teacakes. Sandwiches are available all day and light lunches are served. The choice always includes soup – welcome in less than clement weather! The Wishing Well is open between 10.30 am and 5 pm on

Wednesday to Sunday from the week before Mothering Sunday to the Sunday of the weekend the clocks go back. Telephone: 01323 487967.

DISTANCE: 6 miles.

MAP: OS Landranger 199 Eastbourne and Hastings or Explorer 123 South Downs Way, Newhaven to Eastbourne.

STARTING POINT: Wilmington car park (GR 544041).

HOW TO GET THERE: From the A27, Lewes to Polegate road, 2 miles east of Polegate at Wilmington, take a minor road, signed 'Litlington 2¹/₄', through the village to a car park on the right at the far end of the village.

ALTERNATIVE STARTING POINT: The tea shop is close to the end of the walk. If you wish to visit it first, turn left out of the car park through the village.

THE WALK

There is a good view of the mysterious Long Man of Wilmington from the car park. The 226 foot high figure was carved into the chalk hillside sometime before 1779, the year it was first mentioned in print. Theories abound, from a Celtic god, opening the doors of heaven to the sun, to Hercules or Balder, a Norse deity, or maybe an 18th century joke. The most remarkable feature of this geoglyph is that it takes account of perspective and the slope of the hill so that it maintains the proportions of a man when viewed from below. A carving in the chalk would rapidly be grown over unless maintained. In 1969 it was made more permanent with over 700 concrete blocks marking the outline.

1. Return to the road and take a footpath opposite, signed 'Footpath to Long Man', to meet a cross path at his feet.

2. Turn right to reach a gate and cross path.

If you look at the vegetation around your feet you will see that it is not just grass but a rich variety of short herbs. In summer when they are in bloom, the sight is a delight. This typical downland ecosystem results from grazing by rabbits and sheep and without the nibbling animals, it would quickly revert to scrub and then woods. The animals' teeth nip off any tender, germinating trees or shrubs and prevent them becoming established. There has been a substantial decline in chalk grassland in recent decades. Much has been ploughed up on gentler gradients. On steeper slopes, the threat is from changed economics of farming making sheep rearing less attractive and smaller rabbit populations due to myxomatosis allowing scrub to invade. As you climb, a second carving in the chalk can be seen across the valley to the right (see walk 13).

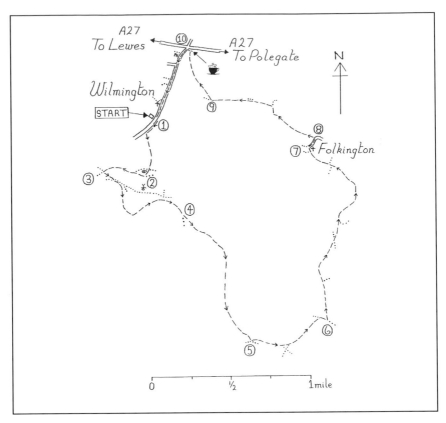

3. Turn left, uphill. The path joins a track coming up the hill from the right. Bear right on this track and continue uphill, pausing to admire the ever-expanding and wonderful views. When the track levels out, press on past tumuli on the left and through a gate.

4. At a fork bear left away from a fence. At the time of writing, the path is not continually obvious on the ground but occasional posts show the line. Go through two gates and into a wood to meet a cross path some 100 yards after the second gate.

5. Turn left. When the path forks, bear left, leaving the South Downs Way. Continue ahead as a path joins from the right.

6. After a good quarter of a mile, watch for a post with red and blue arrows. Turn left on a hedged path. (Note: do not mistake a path 150 yards earlier on a bend where an apparent path on the left leads to a field gate for the route.) Follow this path for about 1¼ miles.

7. At a lane, turn right through the hamlet of Folkington, passing the church on the right.

8. When the lane bends right, turn left by a letterbox on a path signed 'Wilmington 1 mile'. After passing through a gate and by a brick pillar, the path lies along the top left hand side of a field to a gate. Through the gate, turn right to the end of the field. Do not go through the gateway but turn left along the right-hand side of a field. When the hedge on the right ends, go ahead on a bank to walk to the left of a line of small trees. Go through a gate and continue along the right-hand side of the next field for about 100 yards.

☕ **9.** Cross a stile on the right and bear diagonally left across a field and across the corner of the next field. Now cross two small fields, then go diagonally left to the A27 and the tea shop on the right.

10. From the entrance walk ahead along the verge to a lane, signed 'Litlington 2¼'. Turn left through Wilmington to the car park where this walk started.

After the Norman Conquest the Benedictine Abbey of Grestain in France acquired the manor of Wilmington. The Priory was established in 1088, to house the two or three monks who were the Abbot's representatives and their household. This alien order was regarded with suspicion during the Hundred Years War and the Priory was seized by Richard II in 1380 and fell into disuse. The present buildings date from 1243 onwards and are not open to the public at the time of writing. The church was built for both the monks, who would have used the chancel, and local people, who would have used the nave. There is more information about the church available within but look particularly for the charming butterfly and bee window. This is in what was the North Chapel, now used as a vestry and located behind the organ. A massive yew in the churchyard has a girth of over 23 feet and is over a thousand years old – older than the church. It is held together with chains and supported by props.

When Wilmington Priory was active there was a brisk flow of pilgrim traffic between Canterbury, Chichester and Winchester that used the dry high ground of the South Downs. One theory about the Long Man is that he was carved as an advertising hoarding to help travellers find the lodging at the Priory.

Walk 15
BIRLING GAP

*O*n *a sunny, breezy day this cliff-top walk is an exhilarating experience with blue sky, green grass, white cliffs and the sound of sea birds and surf. White cliffs are one of the enduring images of England and the outward leg has views of some of the most famous – the Seven Sisters. Cliff walks are rarely level and this is no exception so even though it is short, it demands enough exertion to deserve a good tea.*

 The Coffee Shop at Birling Gap Hotel is partly in an enclosed verandah, very welcome on a winter's day. There are also some tables outside overlooking the cliffs and beach. The Coffee Shop serves cakes, sandwiches and some meals. Full meals, particularly featuring fish, are available in the public bar and restaurant of the hotel. One unusual feature is that the Coffee Shop has pool tables. It is open from 9.30 am to 6 pm throughout the year. Telephone: 01323 423197.

DISTANCE: 3 miles.

MAP: OS Landranger 199 Eastbourne and Hastings or Explorer 123 South Downs Way Newhaven to Eastbourne.

STARTING POINT: Shooters Bottom lay-by on the Beachy Head road (GR 575956).

HOW TO GET THERE: From the A259 Seaford to Eastbourne road 1¹/₂ miles east of East Dean, take the B2103, signed 'Seafront 2 Beachy Head 2'. After a mile take a minor road right, signed 'Birling Gap 4'. Carry on for a mile after Beachy Head Countryside Centre and pub to Shooters Bottom lay-by on the left.

ALTERNATIVE STARTING POINT: If you wish to visit the tea shop at the beginning or end of your walk, start at Birling Gap where there is plenty of room in the car park adjacent to the hotel. You will then start the walk at point 3.

THE WALK

1. With your back to the road, leave the right hand side of the lay-by and walk a few yards parallel with the road, then bear left up a small valley to the cliffs.

At the cliffs look left for a view of Beachy Head. This is the eastern end of the South Downs where they meet the sea and is the most spectacular chalk precipice in England – a sheer drop of over 500 feet to the waves crashing below. The colossal mass of Beachy Head dwarfs the red and white striped lighthouse on the wave-cut platform below. Beachy is thought to come from the French 'beau chef', meaning beautiful headland.

2. Turn right along the cliffs. After passing a parking area, continue up a surfaced track to a disused lighthouse. Pass to the rear of the lighthouse then return to the cliff path and press on to Birling Gap. The Coffee Shop is on the coastal side of Birling Gap Hotel.

As you walk towards Birling Gap the view ahead of the Seven Sisters is spectacular. The National Trust and County Council own the cliffs so their future is assured. The disused lighthouse is called Belle Tout. It was built in 1834 by Mad Jack Fuller (see walks 17 and 19) and shows that his passion for building follies could turn to something more practical.

Birling Gap is the first break in the cliffs past Beachy Head and was used as a landing place by smugglers in the 18th and 19th centuries. These cliffs are crumbling at the rate of about three feet a year. This process is entirely natural but three cottages have had to be demolished before they fell into the sea and the rest are threatened. Coastal defences can be extremely expensive and are not always

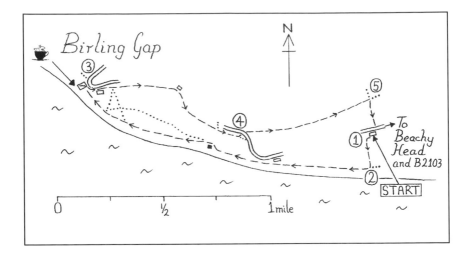

successful in the long term. In addition, defending one area can have unforeseen effects elsewhere. The alternative strategy is to recognise the immutable force of long-term natural changes and allow them to take their course. This latter approach is, of course, deeply unpopular with those whose property is threatened and at the time of writing there are vociferous protests about this strategy.

3. Make your way through the car park towards the road. Turn right on a path roughly parallel with the road that leads along the bottom of a slope on the right. Continue past a further parking area.

4. As the path approaches the road, watch for a bridleway post on the other side, signed 'Eastbourne 2¼ miles'. Cut across to this and follow it, passing behind a farm house, to a cross path in front of a gate and stile. (Note: if you reach the parking area passed on the outward leg, you have gone too far. Turn left along the road to find the bridleway.)

5. Turn right to the road and the starting point.

Walk 16
HERSTMONCEUX CASTLE AND BOREHAM STREET

This pleasant and easy walk starts close to Herstmonceux Castle and Observatory, now a Science Centre, and has excellent views of both. It can easily be combined with a visit to the entertaining Science Centre and Castle gardens to make a varied and interesting all-day expedition. Much of the outward leg is through woods round the Castle before a walk along a very quiet lane – barely more than a track – leads to the welcome tea shop at Boreham Street. The return uses part of a long-distance trail, the 1066 Walk, so it is well way-marked and easy to follow.

Scolfe's is an attractive traditional tea shop housed in a Grade II listed building dating back to 1392. The name comes from the family who lived here in the 16th century. The tea shop's particular speciality is very reasonably priced home cooked lunches, and sandwiches or filled jacket potatoes are also available. The tempting cakes are also offered with sandwiches as various set teas. The cream teas feature clotted cream. The tea shop has a small gift shop area and an unusual feature is a display by an estate agent with local properties for sale – a subject for discussion over tea? There is a most attractive garden at the rear with fine views. They are open Thursday to Sunday throughout the year between 10.30 am and 5 pm except on winter weekdays when they don't open until noon. They also open on Wednesdays in summer. Telephone: 01323 833296.

When the tea shop is closed, the café at the Science Centre serves refreshments.

DISTANCE: 4 miles.

MAP: OS Landranger 199 Eastbourne and Hastings or Explorer 124 Hastings and Bexhill.

STARTING POINT: Entrance to Herstmonceux Castle (GR 653103).

HOW TO GET THERE: From the A271, Hastings to Battle road, about $1\frac{1}{2}$ miles east of Herstmonceux village, take a minor road south, signed 'Wartling $1\frac{1}{2}$ Pevensey 6' and 'Herstmonceux Castle and Science Centre', for a mile to a lay-by on the right immediately before the entrance to Herstmonceux Castle and Science Centre.

ALTERNATIVE STARTING POINT: If you wish to visit the tea shop at the beginning or end of your walk, start in Boreham Street at the tea shop where you are welcome to leave your car. You will then start the walk at point 6.

THE WALK

1. Facing the road turn right past the entrance to Herstmonceux Castle. Immediately before a presently disused parking area, turn right on a path way-marked with the 1066 Walk symbol and signed 'Herstmonceux Church $\frac{3}{4}$ mile, Pevensey 7 miles'. Pass the Observatory on the right. Cross a surfaced drive and continue on a fenced bridleway.

Glare from streetlights and atmospheric pollution obscure the spectacle of the night sky. The Royal Observatory moved here from its original home at Greenwich in 1948 and over the next 20 years the mighty Isaac Newton telescope was planned and built. The domes of this and the other telescopes were sheathed in copper, which turns green when it weathers, so they would be less obtrusive. By the 1970s the viewing conditions over the Sussex countryside had in turn deteriorated so the Isaac Newton telescope was moved to the Canary Islands and the scientific institution of the Royal Greenwich Observatory has moved to Cambridge. The buildings have been put to use as a Science Centre where you can have hours of fun with the

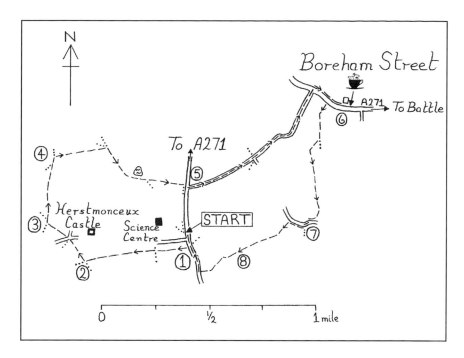

hands-on exhibits. The Science Centre is open every day from the end of March until to end of October between 10 am and 6 pm (or dusk, if earlier). Telephone: 01323 832731.

2. Some 50 yards after the fences end, you come to a cross path in a field marked by a finger post. Turn right to a stile in the corner then continue on the well-signed path over a surfaced drive and a field to a stile into a wood. Press on through the wood to a cross path after 50 yards.

Sir Roger de Fiennes, a veteran of Agincourt, built Herstmonceux (pronounced Herst-mon-soo) Castle on the site of a former Norman manor house in 1440. By the 18th century it had become a romantic, ivy-covered ruin and remained in this state of dilapidation for 150 years until restored in the 20th century. It is now used as an international study centre and is not generally open to the public, though guided tours are sometimes given. The gardens are open between the end of March and the end of October and a combined ticket with the Science Centre may be purchased. Telephone: 01323 833816. During the years the building was derelict, it was used as a dropping off point by smugglers. All over England, the appearance of ghosts is connected to the amount of smuggling. Headless horsemen, moaning monks and clanking chains are a good way of keeping inquisitive people away and explaining things that go bump in the night. Herstmonceux's version was a nine feet high headless drummer who was said to patrol the battlements.

3. Turn right on a signed bridleway and follow it out of the wood and down into a small valley. Go through a gateway onto a track and turn right.

To the left is Herstmonceux Place, built to replace the castle. The estate once belonged to the Hare family. One member, Georgina Hare Naylor, apparently used to ride a donkey about the estate dressed in a white shift and go to church accompanied by a white doe.

4. When the fence on the right ends, turn right on a path across a field to a gate. Through the gate carry on along a path through a wood, passing a pond. Ignore a path branching right and continue to a lane.

☕ **5.** Walk along the lane opposite to Boreham Street, ignoring a lane to the right. Cross a main road to a footway on the other side and turn right to the tea shop.

6. Turn right out of the tea shop and return along the road for 125 yards, Turn left over a stile on a path between a fence and a hedge. Once more, this has the 1066 way-mark and is signed 'Herstmonceux Castle 2m'. Over another stile bear diagonally left. In the next field turn right to walk along the right-hand side of the field to a stile, then bear left again to go from stile to stile across several small fields. In the last field the stile is at the far right corner and gives onto a lane.

7. Turn right for 40 yards then left on a way-marked path, signed 'Herstmonceux Castle 1¾m' that skirts the right-hand edge of a large field, initially parallel with the lane then soon walking with a wood on the right.

8. Some 20 yards before the end of this very large field, bear right into the wood and continue in the same direction to a stile. Over the stile walk up the left-hand side of a field to a lane. Turn right back to the start.

Walk 17
BATEMAN'S AND BURWASH

This superb walk explores the lovely Dudwell valley. It passes Bateman's, the home of Rudyard Kipling, and Burwash, where a charming tea room waits with welcome refreshment. At 7½ miles with four significant ascents, this is one of the more demanding walks in this book. The undulating and heavily wooded landscape rewards the walker's efforts with a succession of splendid views across the Weald. Some of the route is on bridleways, which can be muddy after rain, so stout footwear is advised.

The Tea Rooms behind Chateaubriand Antiques Centre in Burwash has delicious scones, which can be enjoyed all the more with clotted cream and jam. There is also a selection of cakes and other tea time favourites such as toasted teacakes. Light lunches including sandwiches, salads and things on toast are available. The building dates from the end of the 14th century and the tea room is at the rear. The window looks out across the Weald with the same excellent views you have enjoyed throughout the walk. There are also some tables in the garden. They are open throughout the year every day except Monday (open Bank Holiday Mondays) until 5 pm, opening at 10 am during the week and at noon on Sunday. Telephone: 01435 882535.

DISTANCE: 7^1/$_2$ miles.

MAP: OS Landranger 199 Eastbourne and Hastings or Explorer 124 Hastings and Bexhill or 136 The Weald, Royal Tunbridge Wells.

STARTING POINT: Lay-by at eastern end of Burwash Weald 100 yards east of the Wheel Inn (GR 652232).

HOW TO GET THERE: Burwash Weald is on the A265, Hurst Green to Heathfield road.

ALTERNATIVE STARTING POINT: If you wish to visit the tea shop at the beginning or end of your walk, start in Burwash where there is ample parking in the village car park. Turn right out of the car park to the tea shop on the left. You will then start the walk at point 14.

THE WALK

1. Facing the road, turn right. Opposite the Wheel Inn turn left on Willingford Lane for 30 yards. Turn right on a signed path that leads down into a valley to a confluence of streams. Cross a footbridge and continue on the path up the other side of the valley, climbing through woods with a fence on the left then along the left-hand side of a field, to a track.

2. Turn left along the track, passing barns on the left.

3. Immediately after Henhurst Farm, turn right to a stile by a garage. Do not cross the stile but turn left on a signed path. After leaving the woodland at a gate, the path is less obvious. Continue along the right-hand side of a field, passing a stile on the right, to a stile in the right-hand corner. Carry on in the same direction across two further fields down into a valley and a footbridge over the river Dudwell.

4. Over the footbridge, cross a stile on the left to walk with woods on the right. When the wood shortly ends, bear slightly right to a gateway. Go ahead to pass to the left of the left-hand one of two buildings seen ahead to a gate giving onto a track to Glaziers Forge Farm.

5. Turn left.

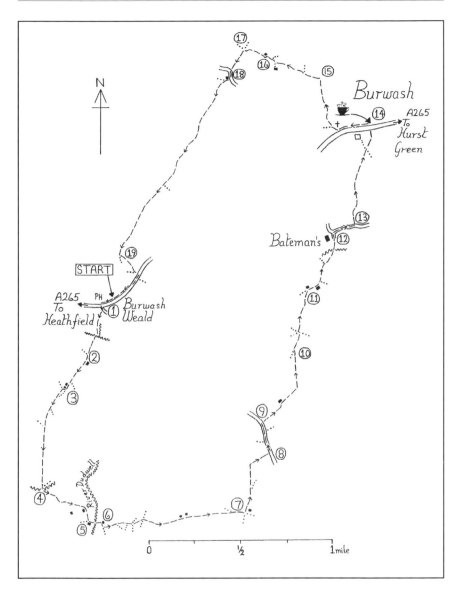

6. Some 25 yards after a wooden garage on the left, turn left on a path that climbs through woods. Ignore two paths on the right and continue across two grassy cross paths to leave the wood at a gate into a field. Bear slightly left to pass a thatched, restored barn and a farm house then continue ahead along a concrete track.

7. Just before a house on the left, turn left on a signed cross path. Through a gate bear slightly left to a gap in a hedge then head to the far bottom corner of this irregular field to find a stile. Over the stile, walk along the left-hand side of a third field to a stile onto a lane.

8. Turn left.

9. Some 90 yards after the entrance to Perch Hill Farm, turn right along a track. When the track ends at a house, continue in the same direction on a path that shortly leads along the edge of a wood to eventually meet a cross path at a T-junction.

10. Turn right. At a cross track turn left for 25 yards then right to continue in the same direction to a gate into a field. Head down to a gate near the bottom left corner. The view across the valley at this point is outstanding.

11. Through the gate turn right along the track and follow it to Bateman's.

Rudyard Kipling moved to Bateman's from Rottingdean in 1902, reputedly to escape the growing problem of over-enthusiastic fans. He made it his home until his death in 1936. The house, originally built in 1634 of local stone by a local ironmaster, is now in the care of the National Trust and the house has been kept as it was when Mrs Kipling died in 1939. Kipling's study is packed with personal mementoes and his Rolls Royce is still in the garage. It is open from April to the end of October except Thursday and Friday between 11 am and 5 pm. There is the usual excellent National Trust tea room, but this is only open to those who also visit the house. Telephone: 01435 882302.

12. Turn right along a lane opposite Bateman's for 250 yards.

13. Cross a stile on the left and follow a path up the right-hand side of the first field and up the next field to a stile. Now press on along the left-hand side of the next field and over two more fields to a stile to the left of a white house in Burwash, seen on top of the hill ahead. Go along a path beside the house to a main road and the tea shop across the road.

Burwash is strung out along the ridge between the valleys of the Rother and Dudwell. It is a most attractive place with gracious, mainly 17th and 18th century

82

houses lining the main street, which is also noted for its pollarded limes. At one time it was a prosperous centre of the local iron industry. As this declined and local people of all classes began to feel the pinch, Burwash became a notorious smuggling town with nearly every family involved. It is said that much of the trade was bankrolled and organised by the iron masters. One such was Mad Jack Fuller of Brightling (see walks 15 and 19). It has been suggested that maybe he wasn't so mad after all but was heavily involved in smuggling and that his follies, which can be seen from Burwash churchyard, were built as convenient points where goods could be handed over to Burwash men for distribution. On a sadder note, Kipling's only son, John, was killed in the First World War. There is a memorial to him on the south aisle of the church, which also has a 14th century iron grave slab; said to be the oldest in existence.

14. Turn right out of the tea shop and walk through the village as far as the Catholic church on the right. Take a track to the left of the car park and follow it down to a stile beside a metal field gate. Over the stile, head along the right-hand side of two fields to a footbridge with stiles.

15. Over the bridge, turn left down to a gate and then head to the right of a house to a gate onto a surfaced drive. Turn right and follow the surfaced drive until it ends at a house.

16. Immediately before the entrance turn left on a slightly obscure though signed path. (If you get as far as the garage, you have gone 15 yards too far.) Follow the path uphill to an orchard. Turn right up the edge of the orchard as far as the second gap in the hedge on the right. This gives on to a wide cross track.

17. Turn left.

18. At a lane turn left for 50 yards. At the end of Holton Farm House turn right on a signed bridleway. Follow this sometimes muddy track for a good mile. There are splendid views across the Weald on the right.

19. Watch for a stone bridleway sign and turn left. This leads to the main road, the A265. Turn right along the road back to the start.

Walk 18
BATTLE

This is a walk through the cradle of English history. Great armies faced each other to settle the future of the realm where today there are tranquil woods and fields and a bustling small town that owes its name and existence to the momentous battle on 14th October 1066. Now peaceful, the route starts on woodland tracks then field paths lead to Caldbec Hill and on to Battle. There is much of interest to see in Battle so this short, undemanding walk could easily take all day. After refreshment under the walls of the great Abbey built on the site of the battle, the route ends with a very pleasant stretch once more through Great Wood.

☕ Milestones is housed in a 14th century building and has a most attractive and sheltered garden at the back. This has a magnolia – a splendid sight when in bloom in spring – and some statues of dogs, which look rather bad-tempered, and a horse, which looks somewhat surprised. The cream teas feature excellent scones and clotted cream and there is a good selection of cakes. For a light lunch there are superb filled baguettes. Some combinations are suggested but if those don't appeal, they are happy to make up others. Sandwiches and filled jacket potatoes are other suggestions and full meals are available. Milestones is open every day throughout the year between 9 am and 5 pm. Telephone: 01424 775258.

DISTANCE: $4^1/_2$ miles.
MAP: OS Landranger 199 Eastbourne and Hastings or Explorer 124 Hastings and Bexhill.
STARTING POINT: Battle Great Wood car park (GR 765164).
HOW TO GET THERE: From the A21, Hastings to Tonbridge road, 6 miles north of Hastings take a minor road signed 'Battle 2 Rutherford Business Park $^1/_2$' for about a mile to a car park on the left.
ALTERNATIVE STARTING POINT: If you wish to visit the tea shop at the beginning or end of your walk, start in Battle where there is ample parking in Mount Street car park, on the left as you enter Battle from the north along the A2100. The tea shop is at the bottom of the High Street just before the Abbey. You will then start the walk at point 8.

THE WALK

1. Take a track leading from the rear of the car park.

2. Immediately after a track joins on the right, the main track bends left. At this point turn left on a broad, grassy path. Ignore all side turns and follow this to a road.

3. Turn left.

4. Just after the entrance to Rutherford Business Park, turn right, crossing a stile next to a metal field gate. The path shortly enters a short fenced section behind a small, grey building on the left. This leads to a stile. Over the stile, the path bears left across a field to a gap into the next field then along the right hand side of this field to a farm track. The farm track turns left along the edge of the field while the right of way bears diagonally left to a gap into the next field in the far left corner. Now head towards a barn to pick up a short section of track that leads to a cross track.

5. Turn right along the track, shortly crossing a railway, and continue ahead.

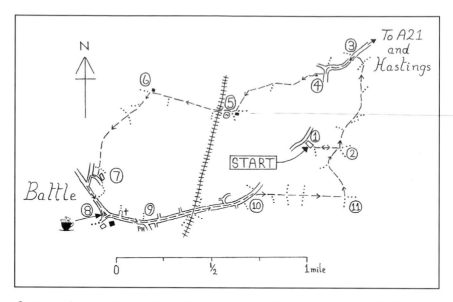

6. Just after a white painted house turn left on a signed path through metal gates. Walk to the right of a hedge to a stile. Over the stile, fork left to a second stile in the far left corner. Now turn right along the top of a field then carry on between gardens and allotments. Go over a cross track to emerge in a car park.

The route has crossed Caldbec Hill. When William invaded on 27th September 1066, King Harold and his army rushed south by a series of forced marches and took up position on Senlac Hill where Battle Abbey now stands. This was a good choice. Steep and protected by a swamp, it made it very difficult for the Norman heavy cavalry to operate against the Saxon shield wall and axe men. The Normans were camped on Telham Hill to the south. We are told that the Normans spent the night before the battle in prayer while the Saxons prepared by drinking heavily. The battle raged all day and casualties on both sides were enormous. The name Senlac is Norman and means 'lake of blood'. Even today, blood is said to seep from the soil after heavy rain; in fact, the colour is due to iron oxide in the sub-soil. Late in the day, the Normans on the right flank retreated and the Saxons defied orders and broke ranks to rush after them. Historians argue about whether the retreat was real or a cunning tactic but whatever the truth, William rallied his troops who turned and cut down the Saxons and so gained a foothold on the hill. The Normans butchered anyone they caught and left their bodies to rot. By evening Harold, his brothers and most of the Saxon aristocracy were dead. The remnants of the Saxon army made a final stand here on Caldbec Hill before making their escape.

7. Turn right to a road, left to the High Street, then left down the High Street to the tea shop on the right just before the Abbey.

Before the battle William had vowed to build an abbey if he was successful. He fulfilled his vow by building the Abbey of St Martin with the high altar on the spot where Harold is supposed to have fallen. During the Middle Ages Battle developed around the wealthy abbey. The market place is dominated by the imposing 14th century gatehouse, still virtually intact. It was built at a time when Sussex was again under threat from raiders from across the Channel and was designed to double as a small fortress. After the Dissolution, it was granted to Sir Anthony Browne, master of the King's Horse. Several of the remaining Abbey buildings are open to the public and a mile long 'Battlefield Walk' guides visitors round Senlac Hill and describes the course of the battle with models and information boards. The site is open throughout the year from 10 am, closing at 6 pm between April and October, 5 pm in October and 4 pm in the winter. Telephone: 01424 773792.

8. Turn right out of the tea shop and walk along the road to the left of the Abbey.

An important industry in Battle used to be making gunpowder. Never a safe occupation, Battle residents made it even more dangerous by drying the gunpowder in their ovens at home with the inevitable explosions. It used to be said that Battle workers did not always need to get up and go to their work. Sometimes their work would get up and come to them!

9. Opposite the Chequers, turn left along Marley Lane, signed 'Sedlescombe 3' for half a mile.

10. Bear right off the road on a track between the road and the entrance to Great Wood Cottage and follow it through the wood. Ignore all side turns and press on along this track to the top of a second rise and a surfaced cross track.

11. Turn left. At a surfaced cross track turn left to retrace your steps back to the start. (Note: if you started the walk in Battle, this is point 2. Turn right and immediately left.)

Walk 19
EWHURST GREEN AND BODIAM

Bodiam is everyone's idea of what a castle should be, with crenellated towers rising sheer from the waters of a moat, peaceful today with ducks and water lilies. This walk makes its way to the river Rother by quiet field and woodland paths and then approaches the castle along a path beside the river the castle was built to defend. The return leg has some very attractive views of this corner of Sussex with the fairy-tale ramparts of Bodiam astride the valley.

Knolly's is an attractive modern tea room behind a house. It has an extensive garden backing onto the castle with tables and shady umbrellas. They serve a wide range of delicious cakes and desserts including a splendid Pavlova. Other teatime goodies include a traditional cream tea with lashings of cream. For lunch options range from sandwiches, including excellent cucumber and salmon or prawn salad fillings, to full meals. They are open from Easter to the end of September between 10.30 am and 5 pm Wednesday to Saturday. Telephone: 01580 830323.

When the tea shop is closed the pub in Bodiam, The Castle, serves food and there is also a National Trust tea room at the castle entrance.

DISTANCE: 4 miles.

MAP: OS Landranger 199 Eastbourne and Hastings or Explorer 136 The Weald, Royal Tunbridge Wells.

STARTING POINT: St James the Great church, Ewhurst Green (GR 795245).

HOW TO GET THERE: From the B2089 at Cripps Corner about 8 miles north of Hastings, take the B2165. At the Cross Inn in Staplecross take a minor road signed 'Bodiam Hurst Green Etchingham' for about ³/₄ mile. Turn right along Shoreham Lane signed 'Ewhurst Green 1¹/₄ Northiam 4' to a church at the far end of Ewhurst Green.

ALTERNATIVE STARTING POINT: If you wish to visit the tea shop at the beginning or end of your walk, start in Bodiam. There is a lay-by south of the bridge or the National Trust car park at the castle (charge). The tea shop is on the main street, almost opposite the pub. You will then start the walk at point 7.

THE WALK

1. With your back to the church, turn left through the village.

2. At a road junction signed 'Bodiam' to the right, take a signed path ahead over a stile to the right of a field gate. Bear slightly right to a stile into woodland and follow the path ahead through the trees. Cross a footbridge and press ahead along the edge of an old orchard as a path joins from the right. Cross a track to a stile and carry on in the same direction across a field, heading towards a building soon seen ahead, to find a stile onto a lane.

3. Turn right for 50 yards then turn left on a track to Rocks Farm. Immediately before the entrance turn right over a stile to follow a path down the left-hand side of a field, over a footbridge and ahead down the right-hand side of a second field to a stile in the bottom right-hand corner. Do not follow the more obvious path bearing left. Instead, cross a narrow strip of woodland to a second stile into a field and go up the right hand side of the field as far as a gap in the hedge on the right. Go through the gap then continue in the same direction to emerge on a surfaced track.

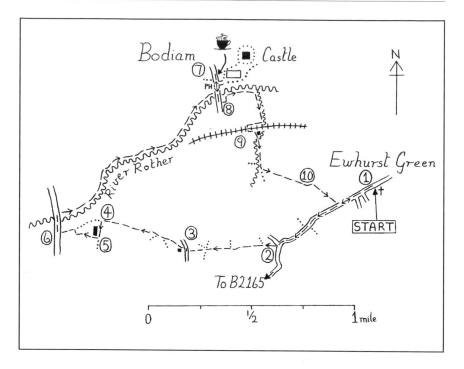

4. Turn left for 135 yards beside some farm buildings.

5. Turn right along a track for 20 yards then cross a stile on the left and head down a field to a stile on the right onto a drive. Turn left to a road.

☕ **6.** Turn right. Immediately over a bridge, turn right on a broad riverside path and follow this for about a mile to the next bridge. Go up to a road and turn left to the tea shop on the right.

Six hundred years ago this corner of England was under threat from the French, who were responsible for many violent and bloody raids on south-east England (see walk 20). In those days, the river Rother was navigable and a possible invasion route leading right into the heart of Kent and Sussex. Bodiam Castle was built in 1385 by Sir Edward Dalyngrygge to guard this route and was one of the last great medieval fortifications to be built in England. It saw no hostile fire for 300 years until the Parliamentary forces in the Civil War reduced it to a shell to prevent it being used as a Royalist stronghold.

7. Leave the tea shop through the garden for a better view of the castle, and to visit it if you wish. Return round the car park to the road and bridge. Cross the bridge and continue along the road for 80 yards.

After the castle was slighted, it fell into decay. It belonged to various owners before Lord Curzon bought it in 1917. He completed the restoration previous owners had started and bequeathed it to the National Trust on his death in 1926. It is open during daylight hours except in the darkest days of winter. Telephone: 01580 830436.

8. Turn left on a signed path that bears left to continue by the river. At the end of the field turn right to walk beside a tributary – at the time of writing this is a dip filled with lush vegetation. At the end of the field turn right again to find a gate and stile onto the railway. In effect, the path has taken you most of the way round the field!

9. Cross the railway to pick up a path just to the right of a large barn. Go over a footbridge and along the right-hand side of a field to a second footbridge into another field. Now bear left to a stile by a gate. Over the stile, follow the signed path uphill to find a stile and gate in the top left corner of the field. Now carry on along the left-hand side of the next field as far as a stile beside a gate giving into a strip of wood.

10. Go across the strip of wood to a small gate into a field. Through the gate, turn right up the edge of the field. As you climb, look behind for a last, excellent view of Bodiam Castle. At the road in Ewhurst Green, turn left back to the start. (If you started the walk at the tea shop, turn right.)

Bodiam Castle may have been substantially conserved by Lord Curzon but it was saved from complete destruction a century earlier by one of the county's more colourful characters, Mad Jack Fuller of Brightling, who bought it to stop it being pulled down. He was the squire of Brightling and a wealthy ironmaster. A generous philanthropist, he was one of the first to recognise the genius of Turner, whom he commissioned to paint a number of pictures of Sussex. He was MP for East Sussex from 1801 to 1812 following an election that is said to have cost him £50,000. On one occasion he was thrown out of the House for calling the Speaker, 'an insignificant little fellow in a wig'. He had a wide range of interests and enjoyed the good things of life: he weighed 22 stones and was referred to as Hippopotamus.

Walk 20
WINCHELSEA

Winchelsea is proud of its status as a town and it has a long and interesting history as one of the Cinque Ports. The first leg of this walk follows part of a long distance trail – the 1066 Walk – and visits some outlying sites. The views are particularly good for a very modest effort. The route then drops down to the Royal Military Canal, a 19th century defensive moat. There is a level path beside it where you can really stride out before climbing back to the ancient town. Be sure to leave plenty of time to explore this fascinating place and visit the view point described on the return route.

The Tea Tree on the High Street in Winchelsea is a beautifully presented traditional tea shop housed in a 15th century building with a 13th century cellar. There is an outstanding patio garden where the sound of the water feature is particularly refreshing. They offer a range of teas and coffees, including their own blends, which may be bought. The usual tea room fare is available, but particularly well done including the selection of cakes. For lunch there are filled jacket potatoes, sandwiches and ploughman's as well as specials listed on a blackboard. There is also a choice of set teas. They are open between 10 am and 5 pm every day except Tuesday and closed in January. Telephone: 01797 226102.

When the tea shop is closed, the Bridge Inn on the way into Winchelsea and the New Inn in Winchelsea serve food.

DISTANCE: 5 miles.

MAP: OS Landranger 189 Ashford and Romney Marsh or Explorer 124 Hastings and Bexhill or 125 Romney Marsh, Rye and Winchelsea.

STARTING POINT: Lay-by on the southern edge of Winchelsea, by public conveniences (GR 904171).

HOW TO GET THERE: From the A259, Hastings to Rye road, take the minor road into the town from the western, Hastings, end to a lay-by outside public conveniences on the right.

ALTERNATIVE STARTING POINT: If you wish to visit the tea shop at the beginning or end of your walk, there is some street parking in the town closer to the tea shop. You will then start the walk at point 13.

THE WALK

1. Cross the road and walk along a footpath by the road away from Winchelsea.

Winchelsea is the smallest town in England and was one of the first to be built to a plan. It is one of the Cinque Ports. This was a confederation of Channel Ports that originally banded together in the 11th century for mutual support and defence and supplied ships and men to the Crown in return for privileges. Winchelsea joined in 1191. At that time it stood several miles south of its present position on a spit extending north-east from the cliffs near Fairlight. This began to erode in the middle of the 13th century but the port was too important to allow it to disappear and a new town was planned on Iham Hill, 'where only coneys do dwell'. The plan was inspired by Roman ideas of town planning and laid out on a grid pattern, which can still be discerned in the spacious streets.

2. Some 30 yards after a right-hand bend, recross the road and go over a stile, signed 'Icklesham 3½ km'. Bear slightly right down to a stile to cross a fenced path. Press on in the same direction to a stile and gate just to the left of a small wood. Now bear right to find a stile to the left of a barn.

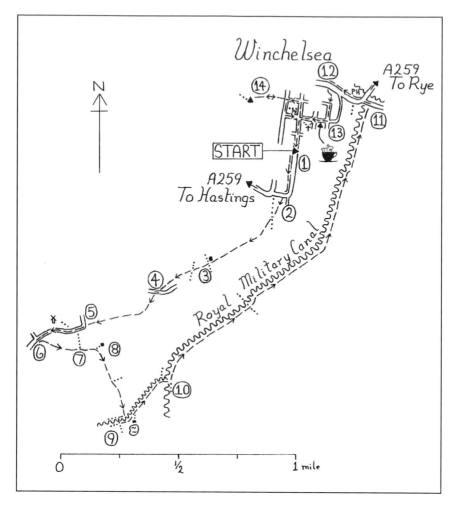

For a time during the 14th century Winchelsea was the leading Channel Port. The population at that time was about 6,000, several times what it is today, and the bumps and hollows in this field are the remains of this bustling, prosperous town. A series of disasters overtook Winchelsea. The sea retreated again and the course of the river Brede altered, leaving the town without its main economic support. French raiders repeatedly attacked and managed to get into the town where they burned, slew and pillaged before retreating. Finally the Black Death led to a commercial collapse and decline into a peaceful backwater. The masonry on the left is the remains of New Gate and was the southern entrance to the town. Walls and a ditch surrounded Winchelsea at that time. When the ditch was dug, an old road was *destroyed and a new one had to be built. This is the origin of the name New Gate because in those days gate meant road. The French gained access through New Gate in 1380, probably by treachery, during their most serious raid.*

3. Over the stile, cross a track and keep forward in the same direction to a stile in the top left corner of a field, and on along the left-hand side of the next field to a stile on the left giving onto a lane.

This first part of the route follows the 1066 Country Walk, a 31 mile way-marked route from Rye to Pevensey via Battle, taking the walker through the heart of English history.

4. Turn right for 20 yards then left on a path signed 'Battle'. The path, across the first field, along the right-hand side of a second and across a third, is clear and well way-marked and leads to a lane.

5. Turn left. The 1066 Walk now turns right up past a windmill but we leave that route and continue along the lane.

6. Just past a lane on the right, turn left over a stile and head for another stile in the bottom left corner of a field. Push your way through a strip of scrub to a stile into another field. Cut across the corner left to yet another stile and strike diagonally across a field to a stile in the opposite corner, giving onto a track.

7. Turn right.

8. As the track approaches a house, bear right on a grassy path, soon enclosed between fences, then on across a marsh to a drain and right to a footbridge.

This is Pannel Valley Nature Reserve, where the original marshland is being regenerated. It is dominated by reeds that can grow to over six feet tall and have clusters of feathery flowers in August and September.

9. Over the footbridge, turn left on a cross path to walk with the drain on the left until it meets a larger cross waterway – the Royal Military Canal.

Some 500 years after the French sacked Winchelsea, they were again threatening the peace of the realm, this time led by Napoleon, and the threat of invasion was very real. The Royal Military Canal is a most unusual inland waterway. It was not built to transport goods or people but as a defensive moat as part of the response to that threat. It was constructed in 1804 and is about 25 miles long.

10. Cross a footbridge over the canal and turn left to walk with the canal on your left to a road.

11. Turn left. At a T-junction with the A259 turn left again, signed 'Hastings'. Pass a road on the left, signed 'Winchelsea' and continue for 120 yards, using a path on the right-hand side.

☕ **12.** More or less opposite the last house on the right, cross the road and go uphill on a signed path up steps into Winchelsea. Continue in the same direction along a road. Turn right at a crossroads to the tea shop on the left.

The path up the steep cliff passes one of the six wells that once served the town. If you turn left at the crossroads you shortly reach the Lookout and Strand Gate, built in the 13th century. The Lookout was the place to watch for French invaders. It is said that the downs at Boulogne can be seen on a clear day and the lights of the French coast on a really dark night.

13. Turn left out of the tea shop. As the main road turns left at the New Inn, turn right, then take the first road on the left to a main road. Cross the road to a surfaced drive opposite then over a stile for a magnificent view over the Brede valley from the site of a windmill destroyed in the gales of 1987. Again note the depressions in the ground that mark the former extent of the town.

14. Return to the main road and turn right. Take the first left back to the New Inn. Turn right to continue through Winchelsea back to the start.

Winchelsea has a wealth of interesting buildings too numerous to detail here. It is well worth taking the time to explore and the Corporation of Winchelsea has produced an excellent guide to the town, which is for sale locally. If nothing else, do take a look at the parish church of St Thomas. As it stands today, it is but a fragment of the building that was planned – but what a magnificent fragment! John Wesley preached his last open-air sermon in the churchyard in 1790.